Augustine F. Hewit

Light In Darkness

A Treatise On The Obscure Night Of The Soul

Augustine F. Hewit

Light In Darkness
A Treatise On The Obscure Night Of The Soul

ISBN/EAN: 9783337775049

Printed in Europe, USA, Canada, Australia, Japan

Cover: Foto ©ninafisch / pixelio.de

More available books at **www.hansebooks.com**

LIGHT IN DARKNESS.

LIGHT IN DARKNESS.

A TREATISE

ON THE OBSCURE NIGHT OF THE SOUL.

BY THE

REV. A. F. HEWIT,

"Attendentes quasi lucernæ lucenti in caliginoso loco, donec dies elucescat, et lucifer oriatur in cordibus vestris."

"Attending, as to a light shining in a dark place, until the day dawn, and the morning star rise in your hearts."—2 EP. PETER i. 19.

NEW YORK:

THE CATHOLIC PUBLICATION SOCIETY,

9 WARREN STREET.

BALTIMORE: JOHN MURPHY & CO.   BOSTON: PATRICK DONAHOE.

1871.

PREFACE.

I HAVE written this little treatise because I believe it to be required by the spiritual needs of a number of persons who cannot easily make use of the larger and more elaborate treatises which have been written on the same subject by the great masters of spiritual doctrine. I have endeavored to follow their teaching in all things, and I submit whatever I have written upon this, and upon every other subject, without any reservation, and in the spirit of filial obedience, to the supreme judgment of the Holy See.

CONTENTS.

CHAPTER I.

Of the Sources and Certainty of Spiritual Doctrine, . . 9

CHAPTER II.

Of Melancholy and Sadness, ... 36

CHAPTER III.

The Cause and Nature of the Obscure Night, . . . 48

CHAPTER IV.

Active Exercises and Sensible Graces Incapable of Uniting the Soul with God, ... 73

CHAPTER V.

Visions and other extraordinary Communications not the Medium of Union with God, ... 81

CHAPTER VI.

The State of the Soul in the Obscure Night, and its Sufferings more fully explained—Directions for passing through the Obscure Night with Security, . . . 119

LIGHT IN DARKNESS.

CHAPTER I.

OF THE SOURCES AND CERTAINTY OF SPIRITUAL DOCTRINE.

I BEGIN this treatise with an exposition of the sources and certainty of spiritual doctrine, in order that the reader may well understand at the outset the solid foundation upon which the maxims and principles of the science of the saints repose. This is necessary, in order to command that firm assent and belief of the mind which alone can give to spiritual instruction an efficacious influence over the will, and thus secure the attainment of its proper end—the furtherance of the health and growth of the soul. The patient must have confidence in his physician, and receive the medicine which is given him with a firm trust that it is chosen according to scientific principles, in order that he may prudently place the risk of his life in the hands of another. If he is going to examine and judge for himself in regard to the proper medical treatment of his case, he would do better to be his own physician outright, and to call in no other. The same reason runs, but with greater force, in the case of the maladies of the soul. For, whereas, in the first case, if the patient submits, though distrustfully and from necessity, to take the prescriptions of his physician, they will produce their proper effect; in the second case, it is only by the avenue of trust and confidence that they can be taken at all, or find any entrance into the soul. In the question of spiritual life and health, one cannot be satisfied with his own private opinions and conjectures, or with those of any other man. Instruction which comes with authority, and produces that confidence which is bred from certainty, is necessary to satisfy a want of the soul that must be satisfied before it can find its due equilibrium and attain a durable peace. As I am writing only for those who have a firm Catholic faith, I can affirm that this instruction has been given, without any other proof than that which is derived from the principles of faith. All things which are necessary or in any way helpful to salvation, and to the perfect sanctification of the soul, are given in the richest abundance in the Catholic Church ; and, therefore, the instruction of which I have spoken is given. The church is our teacher in all things pertaining to God and eternal life, commissioned by our Lord Jesus Christ himself. The pastors and doctors of the church are the authorized ministers through whom this teaching is given. In all matters pertaining to faith and morals, this teaching is infallible, that is to say, the church cannot fail to teach all things respecting faith and morals which are necessary to the well-being of the faithful, and cannot err in anything which she proposes to them with authority as the true doctrine concerning those things which are to be believed or to be done. It is true that the church makes her solemn definitions of faith only in regard to certain general principles of morality, leaving to the pastors, theologians, and moral or spiritual writers the task of giving that full and minute development and explanation of all the minor details of morality and piety which are necessary to the direction of the individual conscience in the path of duty and perfection. Yet these teachers, though not personally infallible, are guided by infallible principles and rules, and, so long as they follow these rules, they are preserved from all error in the essentials of doctrine. Moreover, the supreme rulers of the church watch over the doctrine of subordinate teachers, condemning their private errors when these are dangerous to sound morals or solid piety, and giving an express or implicit sanction to that instruction which harmonizes with the principles of divine and Catholic faith. The gift of infallibility thus extends its protective and directive influence in all directions to a great distance beyond those truths which are formally defined as pertaining to the Catholic faith. It gives a safe and right direction to those whose proper office it is to penetrate into the depths of spiritual doctrine by study and meditation, and from these depths to bring out the treasures of wisdom and counsel for the benefit of those who desire them and seek to profit by them. And it gives security to the mind and conscience in following the guidance of approved spiritual writers, that one cannot be by them led astray from the right path to perfection and salvation.

The principal source of spiritual doctrine is the Holy Scripture. This is the fountain of divinely inspired wisdom created by the Holy Spirit, whose perennial streams water the garden of God through all time. Spiritual doctrine is contained in the Holy Scripture in two forms—that of direct instruction; and that of indirect instruction, given by the history of the people of God and the examples of the lives of saints, but especially in the life and death of the Son of God. Certain portions of the Scripture contain in a special manner that part of spiritual doctrine which is called mystical theology. These are, chiefly, the Book of Job, the Psalms and Sapien-

tial Books, the Books of the Prophet
Jeremias, and, above all others, the Canticle of Solomon, a book which very few
are fitted to understand or to make any
use of to their spiritual profit, but which
is the great text-book of those enlightened saints, like St. John of the Cross,
who have scaled the highest summits of
contemplation. In the New Testament,
the writings of St. John are especially
characterized by the sublimity of the
spiritual doctrine which they contain,
while the other sacred writers are also
full of instruction which is adapted to
all the stages of the spiritual life from
the lowest to the highest. From this
pure and divine source of inspired Scripture, the great contemplative saints and
masters of spiritual doctrine have chiefly
derived their wisdom ; as the greatest of
them all in modern times, St. John of
the Cross, says, in respect to himself, in
his " Prologue " to the *Ascent of Mount
Carmel :* " I trust neither to experience

nor to knowledge, for both may mislead me; but solely to the Holy Scriptures, under the teaching of which I
cannot err, because he who speaks
therein is the Holy Ghost." The certainty and security of the doctrine
taught by these great masters of the
science of the saints come from the
unerring and divine authority of the
Scripture. It is only the erroneous interpretation of Scripture by the "unlearned and unstable," who reject the authority of the church, and, by following
their own private judgment in a perverse
and presumptuous manner, "wrest the
Scriptures to their own perdition,"
which is variable and deceptive. The
Holy Scripture itself is divine and infallible in all its parts, and is therefore
an unerring light to those who are capable of understanding it. St. Peter, the
first Pope, in his Second Encyclical
Epistle to the faithful throughout the
whole world, admonishes us: "We have

the word of prophecy more firm, to which you do well to attend, as to a light shining in a dark place, until the day dawn, and the morning star rise in your hearts."* This occurs in the same epistle which condemns unlearned and unstable persons for wresting the Scriptures to their perdition, and the Prince of the Apostles furnishes us with the criterion by which we may distinguish between the right and the wrong use of the same: " Understanding this first, that no prophecy of the Scripture is made by private interpretation."† The church gives us the rule of faith by which we are enabled to understand the true sense of Scripture in regard to all the revealed mysteries. Guided by this rule, the fathers, doctors, and other competent interpreters of the sacred books are enabled to discern its true sense in the multiform

---

* 2 St. Peter i. 19.
† *Ib.* v. 20.

ramifications which proceed from these principal roots of doctrine ; and, under their direction, the faithful can traverse safely its green pastures and drink from its living waters.

Another source of spiritual doctrine is contained in monastic and religious tradition, which is the sum of all the wisdom and experience of men and women especially devoted to a life of ascetic virtue in all ages. From the times of the early prophets, solitaries and religious communities have existed in the East, whose institutes have been in the early period of the Christian era transplanted to the West. Through this channel, a tradition, partly divine and partly human, has been transmitted to our own day. The divine portion of the tradition is that which has come from the oral teaching of inspired prophets and apostles, and belongs to that Unwritten Word of which the church is the witness and interpreter, possessing an authority equal to that of the Scripture, of which it forms the supplement. The human portion is that which has come from the written and oral teaching of men not accredited as inspired by the Holy Ghost, and whose teaching therefore cannot be received as the word or revelation of God. Nevertheless, this teaching, proceeding as it does from the most enlightened and holy men, whose minds were deeply imbued with the spirit of the divine teaching of revelation, and who possessed the gifts of the Holy Ghost in the most abundant fulness, is not merely human, in the sense of being the product of natural reason alone. The eminent Jewish rabbis distinguished two kinds of divine wisdom—the one communicated by immediate revelation from God, which they called the word; the other derived from the contemplation of the word by the aid of the divine Spirit, called the daughter of the word.

The Catholic faith, revealed by the
prophets and apostles, and proposed by
the church, is the word, to which no
addition can be made. The doctrine of
those men who are enlightened by the
Holy Spirit to understand and explain
this word is the daughter of the word.
It may contain even divine revelations,
as we shall more fully explain hereafter,
and proceed in part from divine inspiration. Yet, as God has not authorized
any of the saints to publish to the world
in his name any private revelations, or
given any infallible criterion and au-
thoritative sanction distinctly separating
that which is divine from the human in
the writings of the saints, they are all
to be classed as human; they are to be
tried by the standard of the public
teaching of the church, and the belief
which they engender in the mind is
only a human faith.

This human faith is, however, certain
in all essential things, and altogether

safe as a practical rule. For the church, by her sanction of the doctrine of the great saints and masters of the spiritual life, although not giving us assurance of the absolute freedom of their writings from all erroneous or inadequate statements, guarantees them as free from any error savoring of heresy or immorality, and as containing a doctrine which is sound and salutary.

A great portion of the religious tradition which subsists in the church has been received from the fathers of the desert. These wonderful men scaled the heights and sounded the depths of the spiritual life, under the immediate guidance of the Holy Spirit, who communicated to them extraordinary supernatural lights. They stand in the same relation to spiritual science that the fathers of the church do to theology. Some of them have left writings in which the results of their experience are contained. We are also made acquainted with their doctrine through the writings of those who went about visiting the solitaries and monasteries of the desert, and collecting all the instructions of the most famous saints which they could gather from themselves or their disciples. After these fathers came the founders of the various religious orders, the great writers who have flourished in them, and others who have not been members of any religious order, or even always of the clergy, whose works have taken a place among approved Catholic writings. Many of these spiritual writers have been solemnly canonized by the Holy See, and others, though not canonized, have lived and died in the odor of sanctity. Their doctrine is therefore proved by their example. Who are so fit to teach the science of the saints as the saints themselves? Who can be better or safer guides in the paths of perfection than those who have walked in those paths, and learned by experience what are the difficulties, dangers, temptations, and combats which beset the way to heaven? Moreover, all the works of those who have been canonized or beatified for several centuries past have been sub-jected to a rigorous examination before their cause has been proceeded with, and have been declared free from any error deserving of censure by the au-thority of the Holy See; while the works of the more ancient saints have received an equivalent approbation by the judgment of common Catholic con-sent, and the sanction of the pastors of the church during many ages.

It is evident, therefore, that, when we read such books as the *Imitation of Christ*, the treatises of F. Louis of Gran-ada, of St. Francis de Sales, of St. Al-phonsus Liguori, of F. Louis da Ponte, of St. John of the Cross, and others of the same kind, we may safely submit our mind to their teaching without any reserve, and regulate our conscience by their practical rules. It is necessary to take only one precaution in order to avoid all danger of error and illusion; which is to read those spiritual books, and those alone, which have been written in a spirit of perfect obedience to that supreme authority which Jesus Christ has established in his church. Those who have been misled by a false mysticism, deceived by a counterfeit spirituality, and drawn away from the right path into the wandering ways of error, have in every instance gone astray, by following their own private lights, or those of others, in neglect of or opposition to the authority of the church. Among those works which are sound and Catholic in doctrine, the works of saints and saintlike men and women are to be preferred above all others as the richest in spiritual wisdom. For each individual, in particular, it is further requisite, that he may find that precise

quality of spiritual food and medicine
which is suitable for him, that he should
select those books which he is able to
understand, and which will give him the
instruction he needs in the present state
of his soul. Otherwise he may misunderstand and misinterpret what he reads,
and puzzle himself with things which
are above his comprehension ; or else
he may apply to himself rules and directions salutary to those for whom the
author intended them, but unsuitable
to him ; he may remain in the elements
and first principles of the spiritual
life when he ought to advance to a
higher stage, and find no nourishment
for his soul in books which are unpro-
fitable to him because he has outgrown
them, and needs a different kind of instruction proper for his altered condition. Practical good sense, together
with the light which the Holy Spirit
gives to each one, will enable a person
in many instances to choose for himself

those books which are most useful to him; and what is lacking in this respect can be supplied by the advice of other prudent and experienced persons, of a judicious priest, but especially of a wise director, who should always, if that is possible, be consulted in cases of doubt or difficulty.

I have insisted so much at length, and with so great earnestness, upon this point, because it is so necessary for the class of persons for whom I am writing this treatise. These are souls who have advanced beyond the first and earliest stage of the spiritual progress into the darker and drearier portions of that desert which must be traversed by those who would attain a high perfection. Such souls are in need of guidance, because they are travelling in a region totally unknown to them, and in the night. Unless they place implicit confidence in the direction which is given them, they will be in danger of losing all courage and sinking down under the anxiety and suffering which beset them. If they are so happy as to have a director who is competent to guide them, and are perfectly obedient to his counsel, this will be sufficient for all necessary purposes. Nevertheless, it is the greatest possible aid and consolation in practising this difficult virtue of obedience, the greatest possible assistance toward understanding and fulfilling the counsels of a director, to have the instructions of a good spiritual book which is always at hand to reiterate, amplify, and explain what the living teacher can only say occasionally, and with brevity. If there is a lack of direction, the book becomes doubly necessary. It is evident that a soul in the state I have described needs to be assured that others have passed through the same state before it, and are qualified by their experience and knowledge of its temptations, dangers, and sufferings, to give counsel and advice which are perfectly safe and certain. Otherwise, it will imagine that it has strayed from the right path and become hopelessly lost, like the children of Israel, who said : " The Lord hateth us, and therefore he hath brought us out of the land of Egypt, that he might deliver us into the hand of the Amorrhite, and destroy us."* When the soul enters the obscure night, it can no longer see or judge anything for itself. It is deprived of that light to which it has been accustomed, and, like an infant whose senses are not yet trained by practice, it is unable to see by the subtile light of faith. Like an infant, it must be carried in arms until it is able to walk. "In the wilderness, the Lord thy God hath carried thee, as a man is wont to carry his little son."† Like a blind man, it must be led by the hand, or, like a person walking in the dark, it

---

* Deut. l. 27.   † *Ibid.* v. 31.

must have a guide with a lantern to go before it, as the Lord guided the Israelites through the wilderness: " Who went before them in the way, and marked out the place where they should pitch their tents, *in the night showing them the way by fire*, and in the day by the pillar of a cloud." *

The first who were led through the desert and the obscure night of faith had need of an extraordinary direction of the Holy Spirit, and so also have those who are called to be great doctors of mystical theology. God gave them this light in order that they might not only walk safely and victoriously over the desert into the promised land themselves, but also guide and lead his people. It is the will of God that we should follow the light of their doctrine, as a pillar of fire in the night. There is no soul whatever that is endeavoring to set its face toward heaven, for whom

* *Deut.* v. 33.

the special instruction, counsel, and direction which are needful for him are not contained in the writings of the great masters and models of the spiritual life. My only end and object in the present little book is to dip out of this pure and abundant fountain of the wisdom and experience of the saints a cup of cold water, to present to the pilgrim soul that is walking in the desert, for his refreshment ; to light a little torch from their burning pillar of fire, which he may take to guide his steps in the obscurity of the night. If I present it to him with all confidence that it cannot mislead him, and claim his implicit trust in the guidance which is offered to him in this little book, it is only because I am certain that this doctrine is not in any respect mine, but that of those learned and holy men from whom I have derived it with the most scrupulous care and conscientiousness.

Some one might here ask if it would

not be better that I should abstain from offering my advice altogether, and leave each one to find the guidance he requires in those works of holy men from which I borrow, in accordance with the sentiment I have already expressed that the writings of the saints are the best counsellors. To this I reply, that it is undoubtedly far better that those who are able to do so should go at once to these pure sources of doctrine. It is merely because I think there are some who are unable to do it without some such help as I am trying to furnish them, that I attempt this task. The works of St. John of the Cross have only of late been translated into English. Although the translation has been done in the best manner, and the treasures of these admirable, almost inspired spiritual treatises are thus laid open to the English reader, yet the work is very costly and not at all widely circulated ; so that a very large proportion of the persons who would read it with profit cannot have the opportunity of doing so. Besides this, the great extent of the work, and the sublimity of the topics of which it treats, are discouraging to many who do not know where to look for those particular parts which are suitable for them, and are apt to fear lest they should puzzle themselves by trying to understand matters above their reach. The *Sermons* of Tauler, another work of similar character, are not to be had in English, with the exception of a select number of them translated and published under Protestant auspices. Even when one is able to read them in the elegant French translation of M. Charles St. Foi, they do not altogether supply the need of that instruction in the first principles of the direction of souls through the obscure night which is given by St. John of the Cross. The only book I am acquainted with which gives in the English language, and within a moderate compass, the requisite instruction on these points, is the summary of F. Augustine Baker's spiritual treatises, by F. Cressy, called *Sancta Sophia.* This excellent book indeed appears to me to contain everything that is necessary, and, no doubt, has been found by a great number to be precisely the book they need. Yet there are some who are deterred by the style in which it is written, and who find it obscure and involved. Although it gives the substance of the doctrine of St. John of the Cross, it does not explain the reasons of that doctrine as he does, and as our modern sceptical and inquisitive minds seem to require in order to silence their objections and command their submission. It is for these reasons that I have thought it would be doing a service to many persons to present, in a moderate compass, and a form accessible to those who cannot get the works of St. John of the Cross, or are not prepared to profit by them without some previous preparation, a summary of the more elementary part of his doctrine. In selecting out of the great abundance of his spiritual instructions those portions likely to be profitable, I have necessarily been obliged to guide myself by my own experience and the knowledge I have acquired of the wants of that class of persons whom I have specially in view. I do not presume to meddle with those things which relate to souls led by the extraordinary ways of contemplation, or who have already attained a state of advanced perfection. Neither do I intend to repeat over again the instructions contained in so many excellent books which relate to an ordinary devout life, and the methods of attaining perfection in the use of active exercises. I aim to instruct and profit those who are beginners or moderate proficients in that state properly called interior, and who are, therefore, subjected to the pains, anxieties, and trials of that passive purgation called by F. Baker the "great desolation," and by St. John of the Cross the " obscure night." There are many such to be found, not only in religious orders, but also in the world, who need assistance very much, and whom I hope to benefit; and I may also, perhaps, be able to afford some help to the superiors of communities of religious women whose office requires them to give instruction and direction to their subjects, and to the younger and less experienced confessors who may have penitents requiring special direction.

CHAPTER II.

OF MELANCHOLY AND SADNESS.

IT is necessary to make first some explanation of the causes and nature of that condition of the soul which is commonly called melancholy, in order to distinguish rightly from all other kinds of sadness that desolation in the spirit which proceeds from the action of divine grace.

There is a kind of melancholy which proceeds altogether from physical causes, and is merely the heaviness and sadness of the mind sympathizing with disease or indisposition of the body. It is a mental disorder, a morbid condition of the soul, to which many persons are liable from natural temperament or from accidental causes, and is to be treated as a disorder or an infirmity, and not as a phase of the spiritual life. The sadness of the spirit in this condition proceeds from its inability to enjoy its own natural activity, which is impeded by the disorder of the bodily organs. Let these be restored to a healthy condition, and cheerfulness returns at once.

Another kind of melancholy is produced by grief arising from the privation of some natural good or the infliction of some natural evil; and this is very apt, if of long continuance, to run into the former kind by inducing a derangement of the bodily functions.

A third kind of melancholy is that which is frequently found in persons whose intellectual temperament leads them to seek an ideal rather than a practical and active life. It is a senti-

ment of disparity between that ideal
state after which the soul aspires and
the reality to which it is bound in this
world, a sense of weariness and dissatis-
faction with the everyday realities of
life, a pining after clearer light, more
perfect beauty, more complete happiness, and a more elevated condition.
And, as we shall see by-and-by, this
kind of sadness is more akin than any
other which arises from natural causes
to the weariness of all created things
produced in the soul by the touches of
divine grace.

I do not purpose to treat expressly of
any of these morbid states of the mind
arising from natural causes, nor of that
common and troublesome complaint of
devout persons called scrupulosity.
I pass over, also, those trials and sufferings which are the ordinary lot of persons leading a spiritual life. All these
matters are fully treated of by many
ascetic writers, whose works are univer-

sally diffused and within the reach of all. I have alluded to them merely for the sake of distinguishing between every kind of melancholy proceeding from natural causes, and that desolation of the spirit which is supernatural. This is a matter of great importance both to the director and the penitent; and it is also attended with many difficulties, especially in those cases where the subject is naturally of a melancholy temperament, and is also made to suffer the pains of a passive, supernatural purgation.

The characteristic mark of the state of supernatural desolation is the severity and continuity of the interior pain, which may have some interruptions and alleviations, but cannot be radically healed by any means whatever. There are certain chronic mental disorders which resemble this state so much that a superficial observer may easily mistake one for the other. When a person

whose temperament is cheerful, and
whose character is marked by solidity
of judgment, is led into the obscure
night, it is easy to discern that this is
really the case. If the temperament be
of that kind which is inclined to melancholy, the effect of spiritual desolation
upon it will be to produce many of the
same symptoms which are caused by
natural melancholy. In this case it is
necessary to observe carefully what has
been the past spiritual history of the
soul. If this history shows that one
has at the beginning laid the foundation
of solid virtue, practised a filial obedience to his spiritual directors, advanced steadily for some time in the
way of perfection, and, especially, if he
has overcome the inclination to melancholy which is natural to him, it is safe
to conclude that a state of permanent
desolation succeeding afterwards is an
effect of grace. This is still more evident, if the preceding state has been

one of great light, consolation, and sensible grace. And, finally, when one shows great patience, resignation, fortitude and constancy, in seeking after union with God in the midst of darkness and trouble, it becomes perfectly certain that the desolation of his spirit is the effect of God's operation and not a morbid condition of the soul.

It is this continual, steady anxiety of the soul to draw nearer to God, together with the inability to find in prayer, sacraments, or any other means whatever that which may still the pain caused by this anxiety, which constitutes the essence of the state of passive purgation or of the obscure night. Every pain in the spirit, whatever may be its cause or nature, which remains after one has made use of the proper remedies provided by Almighty God, and is therefore unavoidable, is also intended as the means of a passive purgation or purgatory of the soul. Every in-

terior trial which is not caused by wilful resistance to grace, is to be referred
to the will of God, and to be regarded
as a means of purifying the soul, and
giving it the occasion of practising the
virtues of faith, hope, and charity.
Even those which are caused by the
sins of others, or by our own sins, of
which we have repented, are permitted
by God, and are to be referred to
his will, inasmuch as it is his will that
we should endure them with patience.
The pain which we suffer from them is,
therefore, of the nature of a passive
purgation when it is submitted to in the
proper spirit, because it forces the soul
to turn from created things toward
God, and thus produces the same effect
as that pain which is caused by the direct action of grace on the soul. The
doctrine and instructions of this treatise
are, therefore, more or less applicable
every soul sincerely striving after
stian perfection, in reference to the

interior pains and anxieties to which it
is subjected. The life of faith is, in itself, an obscure night, and the language
of Holy Scripture in such passages as
these, " The night is far spent," " A light
shining in a dark place," is applicable to
all Christians. Some are called, however,
to pass through a much darker night than
others, and such persons, in proportion
to the depth of the darkness which in-
volves them, and the severity of the
pains and terrors which accompany it,
have special need of instruction in regard to the obscure night and the way
of walking in it. Let them not imagine
that this, or any other book, or that any
director, even were he as great a saint
as the curé of Ars, can remove the
darkness or take away the pain of the
night of the spirit. This is an impossibility. It is the will of God that they
should remain in darkness until he
chooses to give them light. The only
help they can receive from any human

direction is that which is intended to free them from such difficulties, anxieties and errors, as proceed from their own ignorance, inexperience, and pusillanimity; and to encourage them to patience, steadfastness, and unconditional resignation to the will of God. Such help as this will assist them to conduct themselves in that manner which pleases God, and enables him to execute his designs upon them without hindrance, so that they may receive all the benefit which their trials are fitted to impart, may be purified as speedily and thoroughly as possible, and may merit the highest amount of grace and glory. Help of this kind I can promise to give in this treatise to every one who is a docile child of the Catholic Church, who receives frequently and devoutly the holy sacraments, is willing to submit obediently in all things to lawful direction, and who reads this book with a simple and pure desire to learn

how to attain a perfect conformity to the
will of God. If any one who is dream-
ing of a visionary, delusive spirituality,
not based on obedience to the authority of the Holy, Catholic, Apostolic, Roman Church, seeks to find in these pages
something wherewith to soothe and
console himself, I wish him to understand distinctly that I disavow and pro-
test against his perversion of my words.
Such a person is like one who wishes
to slumber when he is in danger of
drowning or being frozen. I would not
write a line to quiet his misgivings or
soothe the inward pain which is tor-
menting him; on the contrary, I would,
if possible, disturb and agitate his conscience still more. The night which is
around such a soul is the beginning of
eternal darkness; it is the night of un-
belief, and not that of faith. Its interior
pain is the anguish of a soul deprived
of divine grace. Quietude in such a
state is the precursor of death, and the

only chance of safety is in the continuance and increase of that fear and dread which will give the soul no rest until it has found and followed that " light shining in a dark place "—the light of Catholic faith. The Catholic reader, also, who is merely seeking to gratify curiosity or to amuse his fancy with a spiritual book as he would with a novel, is seriously advised to lay down this volume, to betake himself to his prayer-book and some plain treatise on the eternal truths for his spiritual exercises, and to innocent secular literature for amusement. I know of nothing more injurious to sound religious sensibility than an indiscreet, fanciful dabbling in spiritual things without serious purpose. I want no such readers, none except those who are sincerely seeking for instruction and knowledge in order that they may turn it to their own spiritual advantage. I do not mean to rel, however, any who are conscientious, and who are sincerely seeking the truth, even though they do not yet possess a complete Catholic faith or a firm belief in the truths of Christianity.

If this book should come across any person of that kind who is seeking for light in darkness, and who is really determined to follow the light when found, I am happy to include him in that circle of auditors to whom I address these instructions.

CHAPTER III

THE object of this chapter is to explain in what way and for what reasons
the obscure night comes upon the soul.
I make this explanation in order to help
those who are in this state to bear their
sufferings more patiently, and otherwise to conduct themselves in such a
manner as to pass through it with the
greatest security and profit. The
greatest cause of bewilderment, anxiety and discouragement to souls in
the obscure night is, ignorance of
the state they are in, and of the right
way of conducting themselves. Let
them understand that their case is not
a singular one, that they are passing
through a state which thousands have
passed through before them, which it is

necessary to pass through to attain solid
virtue, and let them understand that
they can fix their consciences in a
secure position so as to run no risk
whatever of offending God, and
they will be at once strengthened and
encouraged to shoulder their cross
manfully, and go forward, however long
and dreary may be the desert, however
dense the darkness of the night.

In order to understand the reason
why the soul must pass through the
obscure night, the cause which produces it, and the benefits which the soul
gains by it, it is necessary to go back to
the very first principles of the spiritual
life. The end and object of the spiritual life is solely this—to bring the soul
into the most perfect possible union
with God. This union is supernatural.
The soul has no natural powers by
which it can of itself attain to it. There
are no natural media or means by which
it can be effected. It can be effected

only by the direct action of God on the soul, raising it above itself and above all created things. In our present fallen state, this action of God on the soul is necessarily painful to it, and the greater the guilt or number of the sins it has committed, the more sensitive has it become to this pain. The obscure night is the state in which the soul remains, while it is undergoing this process of purgation from its sins or imperfections, and becoming prepared for the complete and perfect union with God. This principle is sufficient to explain the radical nature and cause of the obscure night. Yet, as we have already said that only a certain number of souls pass through this night, it is necessary to explain still further why it is that these particular souls pass through it, while the greater number are exempt from it. In order to understand this, it must be carefully observed that, in the language of mystical theology, the term "obscure night" is restricted to a night of extraordinary length and density, through which certain souls are obliged to pass who have need of a special purgation. They have need of this special purgation for one of two reasons, or for both combined. The first is, that they may be purified from the effects of grievous sin, and from habitual venial sin. The reason why their purgation takes place in this life is, because they are more fervent and heroic than ordinary Christians, whose purgatory must therefore take place after this life is ended. The second is, that they are called to a higher degree of grace and glory, a more sublime union with God, than others; wherefore they need to go through a special purgation, which is not so much a purification from sin or its effects as a refining process which makes the operation of the soul more subtile and spiritual. The soul which passes through the obscure night gains, therefore, two great advantages: it has its purgatory in this life, so that it is ready to go immediately into the enjoyment of the beatific union as soon as it leaves the body; and it is prepared for a very high degree of union with God by grace in this life, which is consummated by a corresponding degree of glory in the life to come.

The reason of the obscure night having now been explained in a brief manner, I will next show what is its nature. It is divided into two parts—the night of the senses, and the night of the spirit. The first part is intended for the purification and elevation of the sensitive or inferior part of the soul; the second, for the purification of the soul in its most spiritual portion and most intimate essence. The night of the spirit commonly follows after the night of the senses, and is incomparably darker and more painful. There is usually an in-

terval between them, as there are pe-
riods of light relieving the darkness of
the whole night at intervals, in almost
all cases. The spirit is partially purified during the night of the senses, and
the senses are not completely purified
until the night of the spirit. They are,
therefore, distinguished from each other
not because they are altogether separate,
but because the effect in one is chiefly
on the senses; in the other, chiefly on
the spirit. Sometimes, the entire purgation of both sense and spirit is accomplished at one and the same time.

The reason why the soul has to pass
through a dark night in order to attain to supernatural light has been already hinted at above, but needs a fuller
explanation. The union of the soul
with God being supernatural—that is,
above nature—no second causes or natural media are sufficient to bring about
this union. The natural action of the sensitive soul, and the natural action of the

intellectual soul, must be superseded by
a higher, more subtile, and altogether
divine action of the soul in God, or of
the Spirit of God in the soul. The in-
terval between the departure of the
natural light and the illumination
caused by the supernatural light, is necessarily a period of darkness. This
darkness, however, is caused, not by a
real diminution or absence of light, but
by the increase and actual brightness
of the light itself, which is too strong
and subtile for the visual faculty of the
soul, and, therefore, brings it into a
state of temporary darkness. It is the
weakness and imperfection of our nature, in its present fallen condition, which
causes the transformation into the image
of the Son of God to be painful. In
the state of original integrity, it would
not have been painful, because in that
state the soul could have enjoyed all
its connatural activity, all its natural
light, all natural happiness in created

things and in sensible communications of grace, without impeding the operation of that divine light which would gradually have prepared it for the translation to a higher sphere. The reason why this is so is, that in the state of integrity the inferior good has no power to draw away the soul from the supreme good. In the fallen state, the imperial command of reason and will over the inferior nature no longer exists, wherefore the inferior nature has to be deprived of the good for which it craves in order to leave the higher nature free to seek after the supernatural good. The cross has taken the place of the tree of life ; paradise has been exchanged for the vale of tears ; we can only return to the promised land from which we have been exiled across the desert, and we must travel in an ,obscure night instead of by sunlight. It is probable, however, that the merit and consequent glory to be gained in the present state

is far superior to that which would have
been attained by the way of original
justice.

I think I have said enough on this
point to satisfy any one who aspires
after perfection, that if he finds his soul
drawn in spite of himself into a state
of desolation and obscurity, he ought to
consider this as the necessary means of
his purification, the way by which alone
he can attain to that union with God
which is the true and only end of his
desires and efforts. This is the way in
which the saints of God have walked,
preceded by our Lord himself, who endured the desolation of his last agony
on the cross in order to merit for his
children the grace to follow him, and to
give them the encouragement of his
sympathy and example. Every one
who finds himself in the obscure night,
and is unable to get himself out of it
whatever he may do, may therefore
clude that God calls him to a high

degree of sanctity, and is leading him towards it by the shortest and most secure road. This ought to be the most effectual motive to patience, resignation, fortitude and courage, for a generous soul. And it is only such that the Spirit of God leads into the desert and the obscure night. God knows what each one is capable of enduring. He never exposes to severe trials any really sincere and faithful soul, unless that soul is capable of passing through these trials safely by the help of the grace he has prepared for it. Persons of this noble and heroic temper are only fearful and discouraged because they think they are offending God, fancy that he has deserted them, and imagine that they have strayed from the path of eternal life into the way that leads to perdition. Therefore it is that I have endeavored to show with certainty, and on the authority of that unerring doctrine which is taught by the saints under the sanction of the church, that the obscure night is, in the order of grace, the vigil or eve of preparation which precedes the rising of that sun upon the soul which can never set, but will enlighten it for ever during the endless day of eternity. One who is firmly convinced of this, who assents to it with a clear and firm faith, and, with a firm confidence in God, submits himself unreservedly to his guidance, prepared to wait with patient endurance during the whole of the long night which is before him, is prepared to receive the full effect of the action of grace upon him, to correspond fully to the designs of God, and to put in practice the instructions he will receive as to the way of comporting himself during the period of darkness. Moreover, he will be able to spare himself all that suffering which comes from wilful, obstinate struggling against God, from cowardice and discouragement, from fruitless efforts to recover sensible devotion, and from the displeasure of God, who is obliged to punish such impatient, indocile children more than he wishes to do. He will, therefore, pass through the night more speedily, with much greater interior peace, and with much greater benefit to himself.

It may occur to some minds as an objection to what has been said, that some saints, as, for example, St. Aloysius Gonzaga, appear to have reached the highest grade of sanctity without ever passing through the state of desolation and obscurity. One who is tempted to impatience and irresignation under his trials may be inclined to murmur against God, when he reads such a life, and may think that he could just as well be led by the way of sensible devotion as by the dreary road of desolation. In answer to this I reply, first, that we seldom know the complete, interior life of a saint. Their biographers frequently take more pleasure in relating the favors

they have received, and the wonderful
works they have done, than in record-
ing the history of the interior crucifixion which they have endured, the secret details of which are perhaps not
known by any mortal man. Those
lives which we do possess, in which the
secret history of the saints is laid bare,
give us the fullest and most trust-
worthy information we can have on this
subject. Such are the lives of the
B. Henry Suso and St. Teresa. Whoever studies these lives will see how
severely these holy persons, although
they had no mortal sins to expiate, were
tried in the crucible of purification.
The same may be said of other saints
who preserved their baptismal innocence
unstained, as St. Francis de Sales, St.
Vincent de Paul, St. Rose of Lima, St.
Mary Magdalen de Pazzis, St. Alphonsus Liguori, St. John of the Cross, and
many others. If there are cases, such
as St. Thomas Aquinas and St. Aloy-

sius, in which the divine grace has been given in such an extraordinary way as to elevate human nature almost to an equality with its pristine state, or with that of the angels, there was a special reason for the exception; and those who were thus favored served God, and merited in some other way to make up for what was lacking in the endurance of interior pains. St. Thomas was destined to a work which required perfect tranquillity of soul and continual, angelic contemplation. He was, therefore, purified and raised to the height of virtue at an early age. Yet he had a terrible though short ordeal to pass through before his loins were girt by angelic hands with the cincture of superhuman purity. Nor was he free from a depressing anxiety concerning his final salvation, as we see from several indications given in his biography. St. Aloysius prepared himself for the grace of God from his infancy by the most

rigorous self-denial and perpetual appli-
cation to prayer, so that he prevented
the need of passive purgation to a great
extent. Besides, although he suffered
but a short time from interior desolation, the fire of divine love in his bosom
was intensely painful, and actually caused
his death at an early age by a real interior martyrdom, increased by many
bodily privations and sufferings which
he underwent during the last years of
his life, in which he was gradually wast-
ing away and slowly dying. Moreover, as St. Aloysius was intended to
be a model for young people, who must
be led in the way of sensible devotion,
it was fitting that the grace of God in
him should have a special character of
sweetness and attractiveness on the sur-
face, in order that the weak and tender
might be gently drawn by it to the
practice of piety ; and that his sufferings
should be kept within the veil where
the more heroic alone would penetrate.

If anything more were necessary to prove that the road to high sanctity and a lofty degree in heaven lies through darkness and fire, I might cite the martyrs who are at the head of the list of saints. We need not go beyond our own State of New York to find these, some of whom were apostolic men laboring in the missions among the Six Nations, others noble converts to the faith from the aborigines. When we read of the horrible tortures joyfully undergone by these true followers of the crucified Redeemer of mankind, we are tempted to think it incredible that the same heaven which they won at such a cost can be open to us. If, therefore, there are any of us whom God calls to make any sacrifices for his sake, or to undergo any wearisome or acute sufferings of body or mind, such persons ought to think themselves highly favored. If they lack courage or opportunity to become martyrs, they ought to esteem it a great privilege to imitate, in some measure, the patient endurance of the martyrs, that they may not feel altogether ashamed to meet them hereafter. The grace of union with God is something so inestimable that it is cheaply purchased at any price. No matter how long and dreary may be the time of trial, it is to be regarded as nothing in comparison with that pure, refined gold of virtue which is gained as a recompense.

Any fervent Christian, who is resolutely bent on attaining the highest degree of perfection of which the grace which God chooses to grant him renders him capable, ought, therefore, to be resigned to the divine will, if he finds himself led into the obscure night, however dark and long continued it may be. If he has preserved his baptismal innocence, and has, with the utmost diligence, endeavored to purify himself from venial sin, as well as to acquire positive virtue, he ought to be satisfied to submit himself to a probation from which the greatest saints have not been dispensed. But if he has, through indulgence in venial sin, or, much more, by mortal sin, perhaps habitual and frequent for a considerable portion of his life, enfeebled or vitiated his moral constitution and contracted a great debt to the justice of God; how much greater reason has he to surrender himself without a murmur to the severe but merciful treatment of his divine physician and judge, who desires to heal his maladies and liberate him from the stains of guilt! Let us take the case of a person who, in adult age, is perfectly converted to God so far as the will is concerned. His sins are undoubtedly remitted by the sacrament of penance. But how shall he obtain the remission of that debt to the divine justice which he cannot possibly pay except by long and se-

vere penances, or still longer and severer
sufferings in purgatory? It is possible
for some persons to take the religious
vows, and thus wipe out the account
which stands against them in the re-
cords of justice. Such a one may say,
Why should I now have to undergo a
purgatory for forgiven sin? Or, at
least, one may avail himself of the trea-
sure of indulgences, take advantage of
a jubilee, and gain remission of the debt
of a hundred talents which he cannot
pay. How is it, then, that he is not
free from all obligation to suffer a purgatory either here or hereafter? To
this I reply that, in order to obtain
plenary remission of the penalty due for
sin, it is necessary to be entirely free from
attachment to the least venial sins, and
to be turned away from created things
to God so completely that one is effica-
ciously determined never to commit the
smallest known and wilful sin. Without this, not even baptism will wash

away venial sin and give remission of
the punishment it. deserves, much less a
religious profession or a plenary indulgence. A general resolution, however
sincere, to avoid venial sin, will not be
sufficient to produce this actual purification from every sin in particular, even
in the minutest fibres of the will, in its
capillary tubes, so to speak, and its imperceptible air-cells. I say, then, it is
doubtful whether you have gained, after
all, a remission of all your debt to the
divine justice, or whether you can ever
gain it unless you are first purified in
the crucible of suffering. But let us
suppose that you have. You were bap-
tized yesterday ; you gained a plenary
indulgence at communion an hour ago ;
you have this moment pronounced your
religious vows, and have received back
again your baptismal innocence. Were
you to die now, you would have no purgatory to suffer, but would fly, as the
infant does, straight to heaven. But

how much merit would you take with you, what degree of glory would you obtain? You would have the merit of the good acts performed by you while you were in the state of grace, and a recompense proportioned to your merit, with a little additional glory as a present from your good Lord. But all the time and strength you wasted in mortal or venial sin would be a dead loss to you through all eternity. Now, since it is God's will that you should live and work, if you are even at this moment as pure as the first December snow in the most secluded valley, you need trial, discipline and suffering, to confirm you in this purity, and to keep you from contracting new stains. You need it, in order to bring you back to what you would be now if you had never sinned. You need it, in order to prepare you for higher degrees of grace and glory. You need it, that you may imitate Christ and gain merit before God. Moreover, even if you do your best for the future, how can you ever regain the time you have lost, the graces, virtues, merits, you ought to have been acquiring during those ten, twenty, or thirty years you spent in sin? It is plain that there is but one way. God must double the value and excellence of your works, by increasing the difficulty of their performance, and by placing you in a state of passive suffering where you can by patience and love obtain that purity which is like gold twice refined, and not only regain what you have lost, but increase and multiply your treasures beyond what they would have been if you had lived a life of ordinary perfection from your infancy.

I have thus far pointed out and proved the necessity of some purifying process by which the guilty soul may be cleansed from its stains, and the innocent soul refined in its temper, as well as the ne-

cessity of suffering for the expiation of
sin, the imitation of our divine Lord,
and the acquisition of merit. I must
now show why the soul must endure
the obscure night rather than any other
form of suffering.

Why is it that the soul cannot be
purified and refined by means of active
operations of the intellect and will, by
the effect of those graces which give
light to the intellect, sensible warmth
and fervor to the affections, by supernatural visions and ecstasies, by the fire
of sensible devotion, and similar means
to which our nature has an affinity? If
pain and suffering are necessary, why
cannot those sufferings suffice which
give pain to the senses without obscur-
ing the soul, and which are joyfully
endured, so long as the flame of sensible
love to celestial things burns brightly
within?

The answer to these questions must
be derived from the principle already

laid down, that the union of the soul
with God, which is the end of all the
acts of God and of the soul in the
spiritual order, and is the essence of the
spiritual life, is wholly supernatural.
This end cannot be attained by any of
the aforesaid means, since they are
wholly inadequate to effect the union
of the soul with God. It must, therefore, be effected by a direct action of
God on the soul, to which the soul has
no natural inclination or ability to correspond, and which, therefore, necessarily plunges it into an obscure night,
in which its natural light and activity
are so far diminished as to become almost imperceptible. In order to explain this properly, it will be necessary
to take up the different parts of this
subject, one by one, in regular succes-
sion. It must be shown, first, that the
different means above mentioned are inadequate, and why; and afterwards,
that the action of God by which he

brings the soul into union with himself necessarily plunges it into an obscure night; and this I will endeavor to do in the next following chapters.

CHAPTER IV.

ACTIVE EXERCISES AND SENSIBLE GRACES INCAPABLE OF UNITING THE SOUL WITH GOD.

It needs but little proof to show that the soul cannot attain to union with God by its own efforts. The finite cannot attain the infinite. Nature cannot rise above itself and reach the supernatural. Union with God is a kind of deification of human nature, making it a partaker of the divine nature. All the active exercises of the soul tend only to make it perfect in its own kind and order. Even when the soul is regenerate and sanctified, its active exercises, although elicited from a supernatural motive and directed to a supernatural end, are in their substance natural. They are meritorious, and they remove obstacles which make the soul unfit to receive grace; but they cannot produce in the soul anything more than a certain disposition for union with God, which must be passively received by an effect of the divine action within the very essence of the soul. Moreover, they obstruct the action of God in the soul, which cannot take place when the faculties are distracted and occupied by outward things, but only when the soul is quiet and recollected.

Sensible graces are given in order to stimulate the soul to active exercises. They help to the exercise of holy affections, to devout meditations, to acts of the will, and the operations of the active life of virtue. For the same reason, therefore, that these active exercises are insufficient, the graces which are in order to these exercises are also insufficient.

Moreover, these active exercises and

the graces which accompany them have many dangers connected with them, and almost all persons injure themselves by their means. In the use of them, self-love, self-indulgence, pride, presumptuousness, and many other vicious inclinations find their aliment, and sometimes the soul is lost through these spiritual sins, as we see especially exemplified in the case of those who are led by pride to rebel against the authority of the church, like Eutyches, Pelagius, and the Jansenists, who became heretics, although retaining a specious appearance of sanctity. The obscure night is necessary for all those who have contracted stains of imperfection and venial sin in the manner described, in order to purify them, and make them capable of receiving higher degrees of grace. It is necessary, also, for all, even those who have not in any way misused the graces of the state of beginners or proficients, in order to wean the soul

from habits of action and from accustomed helps, which are only suited to
an inferior and imperfect state.

An objection may here be made, that,
if sensible devotion and the spiritual
exercises prompted by its influence are
so imperfect and attended with so many
dangers, it is hard to understand why
the Divine Spirit should lead souls at
all by this way, and not by that which
is both more perfect and more secure.
To this I reply, that in the order of
God's providence the state of spiritual
infancy, childhood, and youth must pre-
cede the adult age. This kind of devotion and these exercises are suitable and
necessary for beginners. Moreover,
the dangers which accompany this im-
mature state of the spiritual life may
be avoided by proper care and fidelity.
It is necessary to use some caution on
this head, and not to depreciate sensible devotion too much. Some persons
are liable to misunderstand the lan-

guage of certain spiritual writers who treat of these topics. They appear to think that the spiritual doctrine of those who write for the instruction of persons in a more advanced stage of progress is in some way contrary to that of other authors who write for those who are walking in the "easy ways of divine love," or by the path of active exercises. For instance, they may fancy that one who approves of the *Sancta Sophia* of F. Baker must disapprove of the *All for Jesus* of the late holy and excellent F. Faber, and that one who esteems highly the *Spiritual Doctrine* of Lallemant ought to disparage the *Christian Perfection* of Rodriguez. This is a great error. Different classes of persons and different states of the spiritual life need different instructions; but these instructions, and the authors who compose them, in no wise oppose or contradict each other. Sensible graces and active exercises do not constitute the essence of the spiritual life; but they are means and aids appointed by God to prepare and dispose the soul for higher operations of grace, in case it is called to a more perfect union with God in this life, and, if not, to prepare it for that degree of union to which God will raise it in the life to come. They are not, therefore, to be despised or rejected. Those who misuse them sin by a too great attachment to the natural satisfaction which they derive from them; but those who use them properly neither adhere to them with this sinful attachment, nor reject them with a sinful impatience to advance into the desert before they are commanded to do so. The truly humble and docile soul waits upon God with patience and submission, receiving from him with gratitude whatever gifts he may bestow, and restoring to him with cheerful obedience the same gifts in sacrifice whenever he demands them.

Such a person, so far from being injured
by sensible grace and devotion, is greatly benefited by them; and, if he is led
afterwards into the desert of darkness,
temptation, and desolation, he will follow the guidance of the Divine Spirit
with equal alacrity, animated by the
courage and strength which he has received from these delicious communications of grace. This entire subject
is so copiously treated by several excellent authors in their spiritual treatises,
that I do not think it necessary to en-
large upon it in this place. The only
point I aim at in this chapter is to furnish a clear, practical principle for the
instruction and guidance of those who
are deprived of sensible devotion and
of the power of performing active spiritual exercises, not at intervals, but
permanently, and without their own
will. Such persons should understand
that it is God's will to lead them to a
far different and more perfect state of

the spiritual life, and that the graces
they have heretofore received are taken
from them because, being unsuitable to
their present condition, they would
cease to be helps and become only hin
drances to their progress.

CHAPTER V.

VISIONS AND OTHER EXTRAORDINARY
COMMUNICATIONS NOT THE MEDIUM
OF UNION WITH GOD.

THOSE authors who treat of the
higher branches of the science of the
spiritual life invariably take up the
subject of visions, revelations, and
other preternatural or supernatural
impressions on the senses and the
imagination, in close connection with
the topic of sensible grace and devotion. Their language implies the
great frequency of these spiritual phenomena, and those who have read the
lives of a large number of saints and
holy persons are well aware that a vast
multitude of facts falling under this
head are therein narrated. Whatever
may be the reason of it, these things

are much more infrequent, and, when
they do occur, are of a much less extraordinary character among ourselves,
than in other times and among other
nations. Some most extraordinary and
well-attested facts of this nature, no
doubt, have occurred in the most recent
times. Yet, so far as I know, those
who have the most extensive and long
experience as the directors of persons
devoted to the spiritual life, either within or without the precincts of religious
communities, meet with so few instances
worthy of any special attention of this
peculiar phase of the supernatural history of the soul, that the language of
the older writers implying its common
occurrence seems to them strange and
surprising. It may seem, therefore, su-
perfluous to treat of this matter at all
in a little elementary book like this,
which is only designed for practical
utility. This was my own impression
at first, and I was disposed to pass over

the whole topic in silence. I have thought, however, that there.may be here and there some one person needing instruction on these subjects, and that, possibly, since spurious manifestations of this kind are now so common, the genuine might become more frequent than they have been. My principal motive, however, for determining to take up the subject has been, that I have seen how important it is to furnish a certain class of Catholics who are piously disposed, but not sufficiently under the control of sound reason and enlightened faith, with a safeguard against the deadly delusions of modern spiritism.

The soul which is the subject of the extraordinary communications of which I am now speaking, is liable to the same dangers of which I have already spoken in the preceding chapter on sensible devotion. These dangers are, however, much greater, because graces of this kind are far more alluring to all the

natural desires of the soul, and, therefore, far·more likely to become the occasion of self-love and spiritual pride.
They are especially open to the danger
of illusion. It is easy for the soul to
deceive itself in a thousand ways in
regard to them. In the first place, it
may be deceived by mistaking that
which proceeds from the fantasy, or
from the operation of a demon dis--
guised as an angel of light, for a divine
communication. If a soul has received
some divine communication occasionally, or even frequently, it by no means
follows that it will be able to distinguish
with certainty that which is divine from
that which is natural or diabolical. The
activity of the imagination, which re-
tains in itself the images left in it by a
celestial vision, may reproduce similar
ones. The tempter, seeing that a soul
has received through an angel some
extraordinary impression, and is on the
lookout for similar favors, can easily

simulate them. There is, moreover, an extreme liability to mistake the true meaning of visions, locutions, inspirations, and all kinds of extraordinary communications, even when these are certainly divine. One who abandons himself with self-will and heedlessness to what he thinks is an extraordinary light from God will, therefore, most certainly become the victim of dangerous illusions. He will be subject to illusion in regard to his own conduct in practical matters, and stray from the straight and safe path to perfection into devious ways. He will become puffed up with spiritual pride, and corrupted inwardly by spiritual self-indulgence. He may be led also into the most grievous errors and heresies concerning the faith, and become so spiritually blind and obstinate that he will resist the infallible authority of the church, and persevere in his fatal error until death.

This species of illumination, therefore, cannot be the medium of union with God, because it is uncertain and unsafe. It is a sin to desire or ask for any of these extraordinary communications. On the contrary, every one ought to wish to be led by the ordinary road, on account of its greater safety and humility. If anything of the kind occurs in the spiritual life of one who is simply and sincerely seeking for a closer union with God, it should be received with fear, distrust, and total disregard, and the natural inclination to accept it with easy credulity and delight should be resisted and suppressed. It is, moreover, a duty to disclose everything which really seems on sober reflection to be something supernatural, to a confessor, to obey his directions even in contradiction to what seems a divine inspiration, and never to believe in the celestial origin of any vision or revelation, much less to undertake anything in obedience to it, without the express sanction of a wise director. Even if it becomes certain that one is receiving extraordinary communications of this kind from God, it is a duty to abstain from reflecting on them with complacency, desiring their repetition, declaring them to others, or regarding them as the essential part of devotion and the medium of union with God.

I repeat once more what I have already said, that this species of light is essentially incapable of being the medium of union between God and the soul. This is true even when all liability to delusion is removed, and it becomes impossible to doubt the reality and the celestial nature of the visions and revelations received, as in the case of St. Catharine of Sienna, St. Teresa, St. Philip Neri, and other divinely illuminated saints. The reason why this light is unfit to serve as such a medium is found in the principles I have already laid down concerning the union of the

soul with God. This union is altogether supernatural. That operation
of the faculties of the soul of which
they are naturally capable is, therefore,
no sufficient medium of union. But in
the case of which I am treating, there
is no operation of the faculties of which
they are not naturally capable. This
may be easily understood by a few illustrations. To begin with the lowest
faculty, that of sensation. The reception of the holy communion produces a
delicious taste in the mouth, a glow in
the heart, a joyous sensation through
all the nerves of sensibility, a trance,
an ecstasy. The bystanders perceive a
radiance in the countenance, an increase
of beauty, a light about the head, an
elevation of the whole body in the air.
We call these phenomena supernatural,
because they are out of the common
order of things, and we suppose them
to be caused by the direct agency of an
angel or of God. They are, however,

in themselves, purely natural phenomena. They may be produced, to a
certain extent, by merely natural causes.
That is, they may be the effect either
of causes which are contained in our
human nature, or of that nature which
is superhuman, yet not divine, or acting
as a medium of divine power. Suppose them produced by an angel. The
angel can produce them by his natural
power whenever he pleases, if God per-
mits him to do it. If an angel can
produce them, a demon can do so like-
wise. Moreover, the effects themselves
do not transcend the natural capacity of
sensation, as is obvious.

A person hears certain words audibly
spoken. This can occur from a purely
subjective cause, that is, from a peculiar
state of the auditory nerve, without any
external sound. It can be produced by
a demon or an angel.

A person sees a bright light, a jewel,
a cross, the figure of an angel, a saint,

the Blessed Virgin, or our Lord. This may be subjective, also, as numerous instances prove beyond a doubt. It may be, however, a phenomenon more distinct and continuous than a subjective, spectral illusion can be, at least in a person of ordinary health and mental soundness, or it may be visible to a number of persons. It is, however, one of those phenomena which an angel is naturally capable of producing, and the human visual faculty capable of perceiving. Even if we suppose that our Lord himself really descends to the earth, shows himself to some favored individual, and speaks with him face to face, this is an event which, although extraordinary, is not beyond the order of nature.

If we ascend to the higher sphere of the intellect, and examine into the nature of these illuminations which God may impart to the mind, we still find that it is merely the operation of the

natural faculties which is heightened
by the effect of grace. Let a person
receive an infused gift of music, poetry,
sculpture, language, philosophy, theology, this will be essentially the same
with a natural gift or acquired science.
Even if he is raised to the highest kind
of contemplation, he will behold nothing more than an intellectual image
of God, essentially the same with that
which is formed by the speculative faculty of a mind in the ordinary state.

The union of the soul with God is
purely supernatural. It is a deification
of human nature. By this union, the
divine essence becomes the immediate
object of the intellect, and consequently
of the will, which always follows the
intellect. God is beheld as he is, and
as he is visible to himself, and all creatures are beheld in God. God is loved
in himself on account of his essential
beauty, and all creatures are loved in
God. This union is consummated only

in the beatific state, by means of the light of glory which is the medium of the beatific vision. It is, however, begun in this life, and the medium of this imperfect union is *fides formata*, or faith informed by love. So far as the intellect is concerned, and the light which illuminates it in order to the union with God, the medium is faith. Faith alone can bring the intellect in contact with the invisible, incomprehensible essence of God, subsisting in Three Persons; one of whom has assumed a perfect human nature, and is our Lord Jesus Christ. This divine faith is, therefore, the only root of sanctity and merit, and, as informed by divine love, is our supernatural life itself. By it the soul lives in God, and, as it increases and drives out everything which attaches the soul to any inferior object, this divine life becomes stronger, and approaches nearer to the eternally durable form in which its immortal perfection consists.

The whole of solid devotion, therefore,
consists in the exercise of faith, hope,
and charity. Whatever accompani-
ments may attend and surround these
three acts of the soul, these are only the
accidents, not the substance of the spiritual life, whether in the saints whose lives
are extraordinary, or in ordinary virtuous and holy persons. Tender sentiments,
extraordinary lights, raptures, visions,
wonderful works, miracles, sublime contemplations, are not sanctity. Sanctity
is that faith which worketh by love.
That is to say, it is an imitation of the
sanctity of God, which consists in the
perfect conformity of his will and his
intelligence as terminated in the same
infinite, supreme good. The infinite,
supreme good is God. God loves the
infinite good of his own divine essence
supremely, which he comprehends perfectly, and this is what is meant by say-
ing that he is infinitely holy. The holy
soul loves the same infinite good which

it apprehends obscurely by faith. There
is the same conformity of will and intelligence as terminated in the supreme
good, in the soul, that there is in God,
and this constitutes the sanctity of the
soul. As faith increases, if the will follows the light of faith with fidelity,
sanctity increases; that is, the soul becomes more holy, and more closely united with God. This is what St. Paul
teaches us in the following inspired and
sublime passage: *" Be zealous for the bet-*
ter gifts. And I yet show to you a more
excellent way. If I speak with the tongues
of men, and of the angels, and have not char-
ity, I am become as sounding brass or a
tinkling cymbal. And if I should have
prophecy, and should know all mysteries,
and all knowledge, and if I should have
all faith (that is, not justifying faith,
but a special assurance infused by God
that he will concur by his divine power
to enable one to work miracles), *so that*
I can remove mountains, and have not

*charity, I am nothing. And now there remain faith, hope, and charity, these three: but the greatest of these is charity."**

There is, therefore, no grace from God which directly tends to the increase of sanctity of the soul and a more perfect union with God, except that grace which increases faith, hope, and charity, or, as we call it in theological language, sanctifying grace. Other graces and favors, such as those of which I am speaking in this chapter, cannot be the means of union with God. It is true that God may make special revelations to individuals, which they are bound to receive with divine faith. The Holy Scripture is full of instances of this sort, and we even find that the servants of God sought for instruction by means of these private revelations, without being in any way blamed for it.

* 1 Ep. Cor. xii. 31, xiii.

This may seem to furnish an objection to the rule I have laid down above, that no one is now permitted to desire or ask for these revelations. This is, however, a mistake. In former times, before God had given a complete revelation and an infallible guide to men, the way of instruction by visions and private revelations was one of the ordinary means of obtaining light from heaven for the guidance of individuals. But, since the Son of God has come upon the earth to make a full revelation of the truth, and has established in the church the infallible tribunal of doctrinal and moral teaching, together with that private tribunal of the confessional in which each particular soul receives all the direction it needs, it is the will of God that we should be guided by the authority of the church and of the ministers of the church. He is not bound by this law, and he may therefore impart his own immediate instruction to any soul whenever he pleases. But we are bound by it, and are therefore prohibited from seeking light by any extraordinary means. Moreover, when this light is given to any one, God, who always respects his own laws and never violates order, has willed that the individual should never trust to this light, except inasmuch as it agrees with the teaching of the church and is sanctioned by the authority of the church's ministers. Every private revelation must be judged by the criterion of the Catholic doctrine applied by the legitimate tribunal, which is, in the first instance, that of the priest in the confessional, and, in the last instance, that of the Sovereign Pontiff. No matter how many or how great are the extraordinary lights and graces conferred upon any individual, it still remains true for him that his only path to heaven is the path of common, Catholic faith, and of unreserved obedience

to his spiritual superiors. Whoever
deviates from this path has most certainly been deceived by an illusion
from the beginning, or has abused some
divine light in such a way that it has
become to him the occasion of his de-
luding himself, and straying into a road
which most certainly conducts to perdition.

I foresee that many readers, perhaps
all who are not previously well instructed in these matters, will find themselves very much bewildered by what
I have said of the danger, the untrust-
worthiness, the insufficiency of these
extraordinary communications and impressions of various kinds, for which
they have no doubt conceived the highest admiration in reading the Lives of
the Saints. They will say that, if these
things are so, and the more perfect way
is to neglect and rise above these sensible or intellectual images to the region
of pure faith, it is very strange that

God should ever conduct a soul into a state so full of peril and so liable to illusion. They will ask why God does not place the soul at once in the obscure night, and keep it there until it is prepared for the grace of union. They will be tempted to look on all the marvellous histories recounted in the Lives of the Saints as legends unworthy of any serious attention. They will hardly be able to think that visions, locutions, ecstasies, illuminations, and similar phenomena can be celestial favors at all, if they are justly spoken of in what appears to be such an undervaluing tone, and with so many admonitions not to desire or ask for them, cherish or reflect on them, or adhere to them with any attachment.

This difficulty easily disappears with a little further explanation. In the first place, let the reader carefully note the difference between celestial favors and mere illusions. Only the latter are in themselves pernicious. Whoever follows the directions I have given is safe from these latter snares, and need not trouble himself about them, for if his own fancy or a demon tries to play some fantastic tricks upon him, they can do him no harm. Celestial favors are sent for a good purpose, and will benefit the soul if they are rightly made use of. I have admonished those who think they receive such favors not to trust them too readily. The reason of this is, because it is very easy to be mistaken, and not very easy to be certain in these matters. If such things are from God, they cannot fail to produce their good effect, and they produce it instantaneously, or at the moment when they are needed. It is not necessary to know that they are from God, or to concur with the impression they produce, actively, or to reflect on them afterwards, in order to obtain their proper effect. Therefore, one who neglects and passes them by secures himself from illusion and much unnecessary anxiety, without in any way impeding the designs of God. If there is a question of something to be done or undertaken, it rests with God to bring about such a concur- . rence of the judgment and will of the director, the ecclesiastical superiors, and the other persons concerned, and to give such other signs of his will, as will make it plain according to the common rules of faith and reason what one ought to do. When one discloses his interior to a director and obeys him with humility, his responsibility ceases; and if he is even commanded to disregard and disobey what he cannot help inwardly believing to be a divine revelation, it is his duty to obey his confessor, as the saints have invariably done.

Again, it by no means follows that, because graces of this kind are to be suspected and carefully proved before they are admitted to be genuine, and when

approved are not to be made much of,
they are, therefore, not to be made
something of, and esteemed as having
their own proper utility. They are, as
it were, necessary for certain souls whom
God intends to prepare for much higher
graces and gifts. They are suitable to
the imperfect, infantine state of such
persons in the beginning of their spiritual life, as picture-books and story-books
are suitable for young children. Before
the soul is purified and elevated sufficiently to be capable of more spiritual
communications, it is only fit to receive
such as impress the senses and the imagination. God treats the soul as becomes its childish condition, and leads
it on gradually to higher and more
perfect ways.

There are many reasons why he sends
to it visions, raptures, and other extraordinary graces. It may be necessary to
prepare it for sufferings and temptations
which are to follow by unusual consola-

tions, as the apostles were prepared for Calvary by the transfiguration on Thabor. It may be necessary to recreate and restore its strength and courage under severe trials. It may be necessary for the benefit of others to renew their faith and awaken their piety, by the wonderful and striking manifestations of grace which are made in certain favored persons. This chapter of the history of the Catholic religion is one full of charm and interest, one of the many proofs of its celestial origin and nature, giving it a glory like that of the painted windows in a majestic cathedral, and by no means to be treated with cold and supercilious criticism or disdain, but rather to be respected and made use of, as we make use of other things which are excellent and beautiful, though they pertain to the accidentals, and not to the essentials of religion.

Finally, we must carefully discriminate between the extraordinary lights

and communications given to beginners
and proficients before they have been
purified in the obscure night of the spirit,
and those which are given to saints who
have already been admitted to that degree of union with God which is the
highest state possible in this life, the one
approaching most nearly to the state of
the blessed in heaven.   The light which
illumines these great and perfect souls
is no other than the light of faith, with
its accompanying gifts of the Holy Spirit,
and the fire which burns within them is
the fire of pure love.   They are subject
to no illusions; they are moved and
directed in all things by the Holy Spirit;
and, although they are forced by the infirmity of nature to descend sometimes to
a state nearer the common level, yet
they are for the most part living a life
hidden in God, which is more divine
than human.   God forbid that I should
apply any of the disparaging terms I
have used in respect to the spiritual ex-

periences of those who are still in the sphere of the senses, the imagination, and the natural understanding, to the pure and exalted contemplations of the saints who are on the summit of the Mount of Vision. Such as these are the most intimate friends of God, who when they speak are the instructors of mankind, and when they are silent uphold the world and the church by their prayers. If there are any such souls among us, may God be praised for it! I certainly am not presumptuous enough to give them any instruction, or to pretend to know anything of that high science which they possess by the immediate teaching of God. It is only for those who are beginners, and who need to be taught the first rudiments of the spiritual life, that I attempt to gather a few of the crumbs of wisdom which these favored guests at the richly spread table of our Lord have let fall upon the earth.

Every one of my readers who is a sin-

cere Catholic ought to be able of himself to discern, from the foregoing principles, how perfectly certain it is that the
so-called spiritual communications of the
spiritists are diabolical and deadly illusions, and that any kind of participation
in them is a most grievous sin. Still, I
think it necessary to say a few words
more directly and explicitly on this
subject. It should be sufficient for any
one who professes to be a Catholic that
these things are condemned and prohibited by the supreme authority in the
church. The faithful have no right to
demand of their spiritual rulers a reason
for their decisions or commandments.
It is their duty to obey ; and those who
hesitate to do so, or pretend to follow
their own private judgment, have not
learned the first and most elementary
principle of their religion. Nevertheless, many Catholics have disobeyed the
precept of the church by dabbling in
spiritism, and some of them have lost

their faith and their souls in consequence. Many others are in danger of doing the same ; and, strange as it may seem, there are not wanting those who, without ceasing to call themselves Catholics, consider spiritism to be a branch of lawful science and experiment, give the sanction of their name and presence to the *séances* of its adepts, and argue about the good effects and salutary influences of spiritism. It is, therefore, important to instruct those who are in danger of temptation from this source, or who come in contact with ill-instructed Catholics that are in danger from it, a little more fully in the doctrines of sound Catholic theology on this point.

I remark, in the first place, that all the phenomena of spiritism as described by its most enthusiastic devotees, supposing them real and without any mixture of charlatanism, considered as wonderful and preternatural facts, are nothing in comparison with the supernatural pheno-

mena recorded in the history of the
Catholic Church. It is only ignorance
which makes these things to be regarded as something so very wonderful and
novel. They are like the deeds of the
Egyptian magician in presence of the
miracles of Moses—before the wonders
of the Lives of the Saints. The single
event of the miraculous conversion of
Ratisbon, or the apparition of Our
Lady of Lourdes, with its attendant
miracles, is enough to cast into the shade
all that spiritists can bring forward.
There is nothing, therefore, in spiritism
which is worthy of the attention of a
Catholic, or which can interest him in
the least. Its prestige fades away before
the immense multitude and variety of
truly spiritual phenomena manifested in
the Catholic religion. It is a poor and
feeble imitation—a travesty of the sublime mystical theology of the church.
It is condemned by its very pretence to
be heard, and excluded from all right

to even a momentary attention. For it must either pretend to be the same thing with Catholic mystical theology, or something different from it and superior to it. In the first instance, it is at once stamped as imposture by the rules laid down by the masters of mystical theology, and by the utter refusal of its adepts to submit to the authority of the church. In the second instance, it is still more evidently branded with the divine anathema pronounced by the mouth of St. Paul: "*Though we or an angel from heaven preach to you a gospel besides that which we have preached to you, let him be anathema.*"* Spiritism bears its condemnation upon the very face of it, whether it appear in a guise of treacherous friendship to the Catholic religion, or in open enmity. If its adepts profess to prove anything respecting the future life or the state of other worlds, or re-

* Galat. I. 8.

specting any doctrine whatever, from the
revelations made by spirits and the other singular phenomena connected with
them, they are met and overwhelmed
by the immense mass of visions, supernatural apparitions, revelations, miracles, and other spiritual phenomena in
the Catholic Church, which prove the
contrary of that which they are duped
into believing by their lying spirits. All
their pretended facts can be explained
and accounted for by the Catholic doctrine, and we have been familiar with
similar illusions in former ages before
modern spiritism arose. The facts and
phenomena of Catholic mysticism cannot, however, be explained by the spiritists. They are completely overmastered
by our superior power, as the rods of
their predecessors, Jannes and Mambres,
were swallowed by the rod of Moses.
But above and beyond all, we have a
sure and infallible criterion for discerning
between the celestial and the infernal.

The supreme and infallible authority of the Vicar of Christ is established by the divine word of the Son of God, who has made known his sovereign power and dominion in heaven and on the earth by his divine works, and especially by his resurrection. This infallible authority is above all private revelations, visions, or communications from spirits, and is the judge of all. The demons are forced to tremble and bend the knee, though unwillingly, before Jesus Christ, and their dupes on earth must, perforce, tremble before his Vicar. It is utterly in vain for these visionary enthusiasts to spin their cobwebs around the solid rock of Christianity, which is more immovable than the world itself. Let them utter prophecies more sublime than those of the Holy Scripture, let them show wonders surpassing those of the saints, let them give proofs of a sanctity and courage more superhuman than those of our martyrs, let them heal

the sick and raise the dead to life, before they ask the attention of those who
are the disciples of the prophets and
apostles, and of the Son of God himself.

The defenders of spiritism argue that
it cannot be diabolical, because, they
say, it produces good fruits; and some
Catholics who are deficient in the piety
of faith and the spirit of obedience to the
church are puzzled and made to hesitate by this argument. It is, however,
merely specious, and easily refuted.

In the first place, we must distinguish
between that which properly belongs to
spiritism, and that which is either an
unusual and singular, but still purely
natural manifestation of the mystical, or
even an exceptional and irregular action
of a supernatural power, extending beyond its proper sphere in the church
to the region of darkness which lies ad-
jacent to it. Many instances of this
kind are cited where individuals have
received illuminations or warnings, and

admonitions which were apparently intended for a beneficent purpose. There is no reason why God should not send these monitions to persons who are out of the visible communion of the church, or even to heathens, who are sincere and well disposed. Spiritists have no right to claim these instances for themselves, because they have not occurred in such a manner as to give any sanction to opinions or practices in contradiction to the divine doctrine or authority of the church. It is possible, even, that in some cases, where well-disposed persons have been drawn, through ignorance, into the illusions of spiritism, God may send some rays of a truly celestial light to their minds, in order to preserve them from the evil effects of these illusions, and defeat the artifices of evil spirits.

In the second place, we must distinguish the accidental effects of spiritism from its principal and general tendency.

False religions, heresies, schisms, and
acts which are grievously criminal, may
produce accidental and partial results
which are good. They are to be judged,
however, by their essential and general
nature and tendency. Spiritism may
cause in certain persons a reformation
of some particular vices, or the correc-
tion of certain intellectual errors. Its
influence may work against certain forms
of gross materialism and scepticism.
But this is incidental, and affords it no
defence. If, in a few instances, persons
appear to have exhibited under its influence a kind of virtue and piety closely
resembling the genuine product of divine grace, we must say that their sanctity is either produced by the grace of
God acting in spite of their illusions, and
given to them because they are deceived,
but not wilfully or maliciously, or that
it is a counterfeit which we have not the
means of detecting. Pious persons in
the Catholic Church are liable to the il-

lusions of the devil, and there is counterfeit sanctity even in religious orders. For a Catholic, it is altogether unlawful to judge these matters by his own private opinions or impressions. No appearance of sanctity can authorize him to approve of anything, taught or done by those who have this appearance, which is contrary to the doctrine or law of the church. Moreover, although there are cases where the so-called spiritual communications have appeared to be in conformity with Catholic doctrine, and to lead persons either to profess the faith or to profess a greater degree of devotion and strictness, the final results have shown that this was a cunning *ruse* of the enemy. Numbers of those who were received into the church, having been led to do so, as they professed, by the influence of spiritism, have shown all the time that they were still under the control of an evil spirit, and have, after a time, openly re-

lapsed. In the famous case of the spiritual circle of Vienna, those who belonged
to it were ultimately brought into open
and contumacious rebellion against the
authority of the church. The spirits have
no unity in their teaching. They use the
prejudices and opinions of their dupes
as best suits their purpose. At Vienna
they can feign to be Catholics, in Swit-
zerland to be Calvinists, in the United
States to be some sort of Protestants or
Liberal Christians; but the tendency
and the final result are to destroy all belief in Christianity, or even in any sound
philosophical theism.*

To one who is acquainted with Catholic mystical theology, the diabolical
character of spiritism, in its most specious and marvellous manifestations, is
obvious. It is not characterized by
humility, detachment, purity, tranquillity, sublimity, sanctity, love to Jesus

* For some of these remarks I am indebted to a series of
articles on "Spiritism" which appeared in the *Month*.

Christ, awe before the majesty of God, or anything else celestial, seraphic, and divine. It is extravagant, bizarre, ostentatious, proud, sensual, producing excitement, plunging the soul in darkness, marked by demoniac aversion to the Son of God, and demoralizing in its effects. Its adepts make a show of themselves, and turn their black art to their own glory and profit. Charlatanism and imposture are mixed up with it, and its final result must be a reaction tending to a grosser and more abject materialism than that which it has partially displaced. As I am writing for Catholics only, I content myself with an exposition of its diabolical origin, which is based on Catholic principles, and use only such general proofs as are requisite for this purpose. If they produce a salutary impression on the minds of any readers who are not Catholics, I shall be extremely happy. I leave it, however, for others to make a more complete refutation of this pernicious delusion on general grounds, and for the benefit of the community at large. And I close what I have to say with a repetition of the admonition to those who intend to live and die as good Catholics, that they abstain from even the smallest degree of complicity with spiritism, under pain of mortal sin, and under pain of losing the faith, and destroying hopelessly their immortal souls.

CHAPTER VI.

THE STATE OF THE SOUL IN THE OB-
SCURE NIGHT, AND ITS SUFFERINGS
MORE FULLY EXPLAINED — DIREC-
TIONS FOR PASSING THROUGH THE
OBSCURE NIGHT WITH SECURITY.

IN the preceding chapters I have explained how it is that the soul cannot be brought into union with God by any ordinary or extraordinary graces from God, or efforts of its own activity, which merely excite its natural sensibility. I have shown that it can only attain this union by acts purely supernatural, proceeding from the interior essence of the spirit acting through the gifts of the Holy Spirit, inhering in it by virtue of its divine regeneration in baptism, and under the influence of a very pure and subtile but

powerful influence of actual grace oper-
ating upon the very essence of the soul.
I have shown, also, that the light of
this grace, being the light of faith, is of
its nature an obscure light to the natural
understanding, on account of the difference between its subtile, spiritual nature
and our own natural grossness, so that
the soul, when deprived of all other light,
except this pure and subtile ray of faith,
is at first plunged into deep darkness.
I will now proceed to explain more fully
the distinction between the two divisions
of this night—the night of the senses and
the night of the spirit—and the sufferings
which the soul must endure in each of
them in order to be purified.

Under the terms *sense* and *sensibility,*
the great spiritual writers include everything belonging to the corporeal and intellectual nature of man, except that
most interior and noble portion of the
essence of the soul on which the image
of God is stamped, and which they call

the *spirit*. Harphius describes it in the
following language : " The soul is called
spirit in respect to its superior powers,
in which it is brought into such a close
proximity and union with God, by means
of interior contemplation, that sometimes
it is made one spirit with him. It is
also sometimes called the *mind*, that is,
something interior and superior to the
faculties themselves ; because the faculties are united together in the mind as
in their original source, from which they
flow out as rays from the solar globe,
and into which they flow back. It is
that centre in the soul in which the true
image of the Trinity is reflected ; and it
is so noble that it has no proper name,
although it is described by circumlocu-
tion under many names." *

The obscure night of the senses is,
therefore, the interruption of all that
action of the natural faculties which

* *Theol. Myst.* lib. 22, fol. cxcix.

hinders their introversion and recollection in this deep, inward recess of the soul where grace has its seat, and where the Holy Spirit inhabits. And the obscure night of the spirit is that darkness and suspension of all conscious life in the very interior of the soul itself, which removes the hindrances to the union with God existing in the spirit, so that it can be "made one spirit with him."

I will once more quote the language of Harphius, in order to make what I have to say more easy to be understood and more worthy to be believed :

" The apostle says (Eph. iv.), '*Be renewed in the spirit of your mind, and put on the new man, which is created according to God.*' In order, therefore, that this mind, or apex of the mind, or centre of the very soul, may be happily renewed, those faculties which are called the spirit must be reflected to the interior bosom of the mind, and the mind itself must be turned in upon that which is within itself, to wit, upon God, there sweetly reclining ; and this is to be done by simple intention, pure love, and naked or unmixed actual contemplation. In order that this may be accomplished, the exterior faculties must be made captive, and shut up in the cell of the interior faculties, and the inferior faculties must be introduced into the chamber of the superior faculties, and the superior faculties themselves must be reflected back upon their principle of unity with the apex of the mind, that so they may enter with the mind into the Holy of Holies, and be happily renewed."

The night of the senses is specially characterized by the withdrawal of sensible fervor and devotion in the active exercises of the mind and will, the cessation of all enjoyment in anything whatever, whether secular or religious. The characteristic pain of the night of the spirit is a deep, interior desolation of the soul, which appears to itself finally

abandoned by God, and fallen into such
an abyss of misery that God himself
could not console it if he would.   So
far as the special sufferings and pains of
individual souls are concerned, they vary
indefinitely in their nature and degree of
intensity.   Those who are in the obscure
night will understand well enough what
they, in particular, have to suffer, and
need not trouble themselves about other
persons.   Those who are not in this state
had better not terrify themselves by
reading of things with which they are
not concerned.   Confessors and superiors of religious communities will find
these matters fully treated of in the
standard works on *Mystical Theology.*
I am writing only for the practical benefit of persons who are suffering under
peculiar interior trials, and therefore
confine myself to those explanations
which will be practically useful.   Without going into any detailed description
of all the trials and sufferings which be-

long to these two nights, I think it
enough to say that there is no pain,
either of body or of mind, no exterior or
interior trial, no sort of temptation however violent, no accumulation of different sufferings, and no degree of intensity
or duration in these trials, which may
not be employed or permitted by Almighty God in the purgation of the
souls of his elect. However severe the
trials of any one of my readers may appear to be to the one who is enduring
them, it is scarcely probable that they
are in any respect comparable to those
which have been endured by many persons of eminent sanctity, such as the B.
Angela da Foligno, St. Mary Magdalen
de Pazzis, St. Catharine of Genoa, and
F. Surin. Whoever desires to be satisfied of this need only read the latter
part of F. Surin's *Guide Spirituelle.*

There is no need for any one to examine his symptoms, and compare them
with those of other sufferers, or those

described in a treatise on the subject.
It is enough that one recognize in general that his state is like that I have described, that it lasts a long time, and that
his efforts to extricate himself are un-
availing. I have undertaken to give
such persons a sufficient account of their
state to satisfy them that it is a very
common one, and that they have been
led into it for their own good.   Also,
to give them some general advice in regard to their conduct while in this state.
The first part of my task I have already completed,. and it only remains
for me to finish the latter portion of it,
namely, to give practical directions for
passing through the obscure night of the
soul with security and profit.

These directions may all be summed
up in two words—obedience and resignation. Obedience must be practised
by perfect and unreserved submission to
the commands and counsels of a director.
Whoever will pass safely through the

obscure night must be guided and led by the hand of a wise and experienced spiritual father. The first thing to be done is, therefore, to choose such a guide, unless God has already provided one. When the guide has been found the soul must submit its own judgment and will completely and unreservedly to his direction, although in cases of doubt and difficulty it may sometimes be proper to consult more than one confessor for greater security. The penitent must manifest his conscience as completely as possible at the outset, and take general directions as to his mode of life and interior conduct. This manifestation must be repeated as often as necessary, especially when any new trials occur, or any change takes place in the interior condition of the soul. The directions received must be obeyed without dispute, murmuring, or failure, especially in regard to the reception of the sacraments, without taking any heed to the suggestions of fear or repugnance which may arise in the soul. The responsibility of judging respecting the state of grace in the soul, its general security, its fitness for receiving absolution and communion, the manner of conducting itself in respect to temptations, the way in which it is to surmount its interior anxieties and trials, and everything, in short, which concerns its relation toward God, must be left entirely with the spiritual father. In a word, the spiritual child must act precisely as an obedient and docile child acts toward a father in whom he places unbounded confidence, and who is conducting him over a dark and dangerous road toward his distant home.

Important as direction is, both for beginners and proficients in the spiritual life, it is almost equally important, especially for women and persons of a timorous and sensitive disposition, not to overestimate the office of the director, or to overdo the matter of consultation in the affairs of conscience. Those persons who think a great deal of direction, and are very devout towards their spiritual father, often overestimate his power, and fancy that he is able to do that which belongs only to God. It is most necessary, therefore, to remind them that a director's office is to settle cases of conscience, to prescribe particular rules of conduct, to judge of the inspirations of grace, the movements of self-will, and the suggestions of the devil in the soul; but not of himself to dictate anything, or to control the conduct of the Divine Spirit, who is the true interior guide and master of the spiritual life. The director cannot, therefore, see into the soul, or know what the designs of God are in respect to it, any further than is just necessary for present practical direction, unless God chooses to enlighten him more fully. It is entirely

wrong to seek to gratify curiosity or
find out the future by asking impertinent
questions, which deserve rather rebuke
than answer, and will receive it from
one who is prudent, even if he should
have some special light on the object
of such questions.   Ordinarily, it would
be as inept on his part to pretend to
know anything about the secrets of God,
as it is foolish for the penitent to ask
questions about them.   It is wrong, also,
to expect relief from pain and sorrow
through direction.   The director's office
is to remove scruples and encourage his
penitent to confide in God; but not to
take away the pain which God inflicts.
God alone can do that, and it is frequently the case that the effort to obtain
consolation or relief in the confessional
only plunges the soul into deeper per-
plexity and sadness.   A penitent ought
not, therefore, to resort to direction
with a view of obtaining relief from the
weight of his cross, or finding out some

way of recovering the sensible devotion which he has lost.

Neither ought one to overdo direction by perpetually bringing forward the same questions, the same explanations of his interior, the same anxieties and troubles, and making thus a perpetual and useless conference about his interior condition. Direction should be sought for with a simple and pure intention, not for human solace, not for the pleasure of having a sympathizing friend or confidant, but merely in order to place and keep the conscience in the straight road to perfection, and to ascertain the will of God. Except when special direction is necessary, confession ought to be very short, just enough to answer the requirements of the sacrament, very quiet and composed. There should be no complaining, no fretfulness, none of the behavior of a restless child or an impatient invalid. It should be left to the discretion of the confessor to give counsel whenever he thinks proper to do so, and, if he is silent, the penitent ought to go away perfectly satisfied. It is to Jesus Christ in the Blessed Sacrament, and to the Holy Spirit in the soul, that one ought to go for strength and consolation, rather than to any man, though he be the minister of God, and even if he be a saint. Whoever acts in this manner will be sure of receiving, through the Sacrament of Penance and the counsel of a director, the greatest possible benefit; for the Holy Spirit will enlighten both the director and the penitent, and communicate special graces through the sacrament received with such a pure intention. Unhappily, many penitents commit more faults in the tribunal of penance than in any other place, by acting in a manner contrary to that here described, and are consequently more disturbed and disquieted than benefited by their confessions. There are some persons, however, so tender, delicate, sensitive, and timorous, that they need the same gentle, patient, and unwearied care that an infant receives from its mother. There are, also, others whose sufferings are so acute and unbearable, and whose minds are so terror-stricken, that they are like sick persons, unable to remain quiet a moment or to suppress their cries. They are not to be blamed ; and although a director will be able to give them very little relief, as a physician or nurse is often unable to relieve the sick patient, yet they naturally and properly have recourse to him, and are not to be repelled or rebuked for doing so ; but, on the contrary, to be soothed and comforted as much as possible, until God is pleased to relieve their sufferings or to give them more patience. Obedience is to be learned by degrees, and one who is so happy as to have a wise director will be led by him gradually and kindly, but firmly, through its easier lessons to those which are more difficult. It is indispensable, however, that neither the director nor the penitent should rest satisfied until its perfection has been attained; for until that result is reached, nothing effectual can be done toward establishing the soul in that solid interior peace which is the basis of all perfection, and the condition without which the Holy Spirit cannot reign in the interior sanctuary of the mind.

One who cannot find a suitable director ought, if possible, at least once, or at intervals, to take some trouble to seek out a religious, or some other priest, who is experienced in direction, in order to reserve that counsel which may supply the lack of continual direction. In such a case, it is better to make no disclosure whatever of the interior state in ordinary confessions, except just that which is necessary to sacramental confession, and to rely on books and the interior guidance of the Holy

Spirit for the remainder. God will not fail to give such persons a special light to direct them in their obscurities, since they are deprived, without their own fault, of the ordinary means which he has appointed.

Resignation to the will of God is simply the spirit of obedience carried into the direct and immediate relation of the soul with its Creator and Sovereign Lord. It is to be practised by ceasing to struggle after relief from trials and temptations; ceasing to importune God for the restoration of his sensible gifts and favors; ceasing all effort to recover the state of active and affective devotion, and submitting quietly to the action of the Holy Spirit upon the soul. This resignation ought to be complete, unreserved, and constant. The soul should become as passive in God's hand as the clay in the hand of the moulder. It should accept willingly all the pain and desolation which may

await it in the time to come, no matter
how long and wearisome it may be;
accept that kind of death which God
has decreed for it, the purgatory that is
to follow, and abandon its eternal des-
tiny entirely into God's hands.   This is
the obedience unto death, even the death
of the cross, which our Lord practised,
and by which he redeemed the world.
The faithful soul should follow him in
this path of obedience, without looking
back or swerving for an instant, but
looking only forward, and fixing its
eyes upon the glorious footsteps he has
left in the desert which he once trod,
and over which his followers are now
journeying toward the promised land.

Whoever follows these directions
will pass securely through the obscure
night, and will become purified even to
the very depths of his spirit.   It is only
by this passive purgation that the spirit
itself can be purified from all self-love and
attachment to created things, and thus

made fit to be transformed inwardly, and made one with the Spirit of God. Those who finish their purgation in this life pass into a state of interior peace, tranquillity, and light, which, in its highest degrees, is almost a beginning of the life of the blessed in heaven. Those who are not favored by God in this life with these foretastes of heaven are, nevertheless, raised to a high degree of virtue and merit, and reserved for a very exalted height of glory in the kingdom of God. If the soul remains in the obscure night until death, its death is secure, and welcome to it as a happy release from suffering; its purgatory is short and light, and the beatitude which awaits it is proportioned to the length and severity of the trials it has surmounted, the pains it has endured, and the temptations over which it has triumphed.

It may seem that this road is too hard and dreary, and that, instead of pointing out a way out of darkness and suf-

fering to light and peace, I have only
shown the impossibility of obtaining
either the one or the other. If any one
think so, let him remember that I have
not sought to lead any one who is going
on piously in an easier way into this
steep and dark road.   I am only direct-
ing those who find themselves already
in it how they may go forward securely and courageously.   The darkness
and suffering are already present, and
the return to an easier and more delightful road is impossible. If the courage of any one fails him when he thinks
of following my directions, his difficulties will not be removed, but rather increased, by neglecting to follow them.
He may expect to remain all his life in
the same state in which he is now, to be
harassed and terrified at the hour of
death by the same fear and distress
which overwhelm him at present, and
to pass out of this life into the deeper
and longer night of purgatory, there to

languish and sigh after that union with God which might have been attained in this life, and consummated speedily after death, if he had exercised more courage and fortitude. Complete and unreserved resignation to the will of God, and resolution to follow willingly his guidance, will alleviate suffering, tranquillize the spirit, shorten the time of probation, and greatly increase the virtue and merit which may be gained here, as well as the reward which is to follow hereafter. There are some generous and heroic souls, I am persuaded, who will find this way of obedience and resignation to be just the one in which they desire to be directed, and it is only such as these that I have either hoped or intended to assist by this little book. They will be able to understand now that which I have been endeavoring to explain all along—what is the nature and the salutary effect of the pain of purgation to which the

soul is subjected during the obscure
night.

During the night of the senses, but
more especially during the night of
the spirit, the soul is purified by an
operation of grace, in which it is chiefly passive, from those impediments
to union with God, which no active
efforts or impulse of the grace of
sensible devotion can remove, even
when they are not increased by any
perversity of the will.   This union
with God, as I have explained, is purely supernatural.   It is not a union of
the intellect, or imagination, or sensible
affections, with any form which repre-
sents either things celestial or God to
the soul, in the manner of an image reflected in the mind's natural mirror.
Therefore, it cannot be produced by meditation, active exercises of piety or virtue, imaginary visions, or sensible graces.
It is a union of the faculties and of the
irit itself with the pure essence of

God through the Holy Spirit, who is the uniting principle of the Persons of the Blessed Trinity with each other, of the human with the divine nature in Jesus Christ, and of holy angels and men with God. The beginning of this union in a soul which is not prepared for it necessarily plunges it into darkness, just as bright light blinds the eyes which are too weak or diseased to bear it. The intimate presence of God to the soul, although of its own nature illuminating and beatifying, causes it to be sensible of its own weak and diseased condition. The rushlights of the senses are extinguished by the radiance of the divine sunlight, and the soul, no longer able to see by these rushlights, and unable to endure the divine rays, becomes for a time blind. The attraction of divine love destroys all the attraction of inferior objects, even the inferior manifestations of God in his works or his gifts. At the same time, the soul is unable to attain to the supreme good on account of its intrinsic unfitness for union with it. It is, therefore, overwhelmed with pain and suffering, sunk in its own misery and nothingness, and like a captive shut up in a lonesome, noisome, and dark dungeon. It is not, therefore, God who torments the soul, but the miseries of the soul which torment it, on account of the presence of God which it is unfit to enjoy, and which makes it incapable of finding solace elsewhere. In this dark struggle with itself, the soul dies a long, lingering death, a protracted crucifixion, and is buried, and descends even into hell. Self-love is destroyed, sin is eradicated, and the dull, opaque ore of the spiritual substance is changed into pure, translucent gold. Finding no longer an impediment in his way, God unites himself to the human spirit by a perfect and inseparable union, which awaits only the severance of the bond which

confines it in a mortal body to be consummated for eternity.

We are now prepared to understand
more clearly what is the cause and nature of the obscure night in which the
soul necessarily exists when it is no
longer directed by any other light than
that of faith. I have, in the foregoing
treatise, included a great many sufferings, anxieties, and trials of the senses
and the spirit in the obscure night.
These are things which accompany the
obscuration of the natural light of the
soul, caused by the increase of the supernatural light, and constitute the passive purgation which is necessary to
make it fully receptive of the pure, obscure illumination of faith. But they
are not properly the obscure night itself, as this is explained by St. John of
the Cross. The state of obscuration,
called the night of the soul, in its own
intrinsic nature, is simply the state in
which the spirit is totally absorbed in

contemplating God as he is, in his invisible, incomprehensible essence, by means of the light of faith, which is, of its own nature, an obscure light. A perfectly pure soul, worthy to be admitted into heaven immediately, is, nevertheless, of necessity in the obscure night, so long as it is detained from the vision of God. The reason is, that the soul, by its natural powers, sees God only through the medium of creatures, and by its supernatural powers sees him only obscurely and by faith, so long as these supernatural powers have not been made capable of clear intuition of the divine essence by the *lumen gloriæ*, the light of glory. The soul is, so to speak, surrounded by a cloud, which remains obscure so long as life lasts, but after death is made luminous. This cloud is sometimes, in the case of the most favored saints, illuminated by certain rays of light darting from the ʲlendor of God upon the soul, and giv-

ing it foretastes of the beatific vision.
Such favors are not to be looked for,
however, or desired, or asked for.
The safest and happiest state to which
any one is permitted to aspire in this
life, is that described by St. John of the
Cross in his well-known Canticle:

THE OBSCURE NIGHT OF THE SOUL.

I.

IN an obscure night,
With anxious love inflamed,
  O happy lot!
Forth unobserved I went,
My house being now at rest.

II.

In darkness and security,
By the secret ladder, disguised,
  O happy lot!
In darkness and concealment,
My house being now at rest.

III.

In that happy night,
In secret, seen of none;
   Seeing naught myself—
Without other light or guide,
Save that which in my heart was burning.

IV.

That light guided me
More surely than the noonday sun
   To the place where he was waiting for me,
Whom I knew well,
And where none but he appeared.

The same sentiments were expressed long ago by the inspired psalmist David, when he wrote, probably when he was wandering through the deserts of Ziph and Engaddi: "The Lord ruleth me: and I shall want nothing. He hath set me in a place of pasture. He hath brought me to refreshing water. He hath converted my soul. He hath led me on the paths of justice, for his own name's sake. *For though I should walk*

*in the midst of the shadow of death, I will
fear no evils, for thou art with me.* Thy
rod and thy staff, they have comforted
me."*

This happy state is attained by the
soul that is perfectly resigned to the
will of God, and has renounced everything, even the gifts of God, in order to
seek him alone. The way to attain it
I have already pointed out, in the reso-
lute and persevering effort to practise
obedience and resignation; no matter
how long and wearisome the time may
be, during which it is requisite to endure the trials and sufferings of that
passive purgation, which will make the
soul fit to enjoy the unalterable peace
and tranquillity of union with God.
Whoever desires to reach this state of
tranquillity must, therefore, renounce
once for all, all efforts to recover the
grace of sensible devotion. If this

* Psalm xxii. 1-4.

grace is given by God from time to time, as it ordinarily is, it should be accepted with gratitude as a slight refreshment from the fatigue and hardships of the journey, but with a firm conviction that it will be only transient. The effort to recover the habit of meditation and active exercises in mental prayer must also be renounced with equal constancy. The soul must content itself to remain in the state of desolation, aridity, temptation, and apparent abandonment of God, conscious of its own helplessness, and unable to perceive any signs of succor from the grace of God. When the poor soul comes into this state, it is like a sailor leaving the warm, tropical seas, with his summer clothing on, and suddenly overtaken by one of those bitterly cold and violent tempests which betoken the approaching rigor and hardships of a long, stormy passage around the Cape. This, he well knows, is only the beginning of his sorrows. Month after month he must struggle against winds and waves, one tempest only preparing the way for another, in wet and cold, in labors and night-watches, bereft of sleep, and sustained by the hardest fare, danger and death staring him in the face every instant, and with only rare and short intervals of comparative calm and unbroken repose. The bravest and most weather-beaten seamen often lose all buoyancy of spirit in such circumstances, and begin to think and say that they will never see port again. Yet there is but one thing to be done—to sail on while the ship holds together. To return again to the tropical seas is not to be thought of; to make a landfall on the route is impossible; the only hope of gaining port is to proceed onward in the storm. After six, or twelve, or eighteen months, the tempest-tossed ship approaches her haven, she is put in order for entering her port in triumph, and hilarity once more reigns among her company. "O poor little one! tossed with tempest, without all comfort,"* it is vain to sigh for the smooth, delightful sea and climate which you have left behind. You have embarked on the voyage to eternal life, and you must keep on or be engulfed in the waves. There is only one way to the haven of peace, and that is over the tempestuous waters. Act, therefore, in your spiritual difficulties and trials, as you would be compelled to act, however delicate and timid you might be in your natural disposition, if you were embarked in a ship for a passage like that I have described. Were you returning to a pleasant home, to a beloved spouse, to revered parents from whom you had been long separated, after years passed among strangers and in toil and danger, to enjoy the fruits of your labors

* Isa. liv. 11.

in tranquillity and happiness, you would contrive to keep your courage up during your voyage. On your safe arrival in tranquil waters, and at the sight of the spires of your native city, you would feel yourself repaid for all your hardships, and have nothing more to wish for except to find yourself at home in your own house, in the embrace of your family, and partaking of the festive repast of reunion. In like manner, if you can only attain the state of interior peace which is given to those who struggle manfully through the difficulties of the spiritual life; you will be repaid for your trials and sufferings by the consciousness that you are now ready to step on the shore of eternal life, and go to the embrace of your Father, to remain in your true home for ever; as soon as the frail, shattered vessel of the body, in which you have been tossed on the waves of time, is laid up in the quiet earth, and your soul set

free from its long, wearisome imprison-
ment within the narrow walls. How
much better this is, than to be cast
ashore half-drowned on a broken plank,
a thousand miles from home, through
your own cowardice or want of vigil-
ance and courage during the tempests
of the voyage !

The great advantage which is gained
by passing through the obscure night
with fortitude and resignation consists
in this: that the soul passes through its
purgatory in this life, acquires an incon-
ceivable degree of merit and glory, goes
through the pains and sorrows of death
by anticipation; and is, therefore, already
so detached from all created things at
the moment of its departure, that it has
only to shut its bodily eyes on the visible
world, to open them a moment after on
the light of the divine essence ; and to
continue in a more perfect manner in
heaven that life in God which in this
world had already superseded its natural

life. This happiness is completely verified only in those who are entirely purified and elevated to a perfect union with
God. But it is more or less verified
according to the proportion of grace
and fidelity in those who approximate
to the blessed state of the saints. The
pain of death is diminished, purgatory
is alleviated and shortened, and glory
increased, according to the measure of
the purification which each one has
attained by his obedience and resignation. The essential union with God
subsists in all who are in the state of
grace; even infants, and those newly
regenerated in baptism who have had
no time to gain any merit; and in the
most imperfect. Those who are free
from all sin and obligation to undergo
punishment for sin, even if they possess
nothing acquired by their own efforts,
pass to the state of supernatural union
with God at once, if the soul is separated from the body by death. The

latent and dormant principle of life
which they possess, as a quality of the
essence of the soul, springs into activity
as soon as it is transferred to its proper
sphere.   It is only the lowest degree of
beatitude and glory, however, which is
given to them.   All those who gain
heaven by the use of their reason and
free-will, through the exercise of faith,
hape, and charity, pass through a certain amount of trial and probation; their
condition on the earth is essentially an
obscure night; and they acquire a certain degree of active union with God.
If they are comparatively sinless, and
yet have but little work or suffering
exacted of them, their purgatory is
also comparatively light and short; and
their glory in heaven is merely superior
to that of infants, in so far as they have
acquired merit by their fidelity to the
grace they have received.   Those who
have committed many venial or mortal
sins, from which they have not been

purged in this life, have their obscure night and passive purgation during a very long and severe period of suffering after death. The special advantage, therefore, gained by those who pass through that long night of dense darkness and desolation, with its trials and sufferings, its active and passive probation, its deserts and burning flames, its conflicts and temptations, its mystical death and burial, its resurrection and transformation, is, as I have explained throughout the whole course of this treatise, that sin and indebtedness to the divine justice, when they exist, are expiated in this world, and that the soul is fitted for the higher degrees of glory and beatitude. Some one of the countless degrees of celestial splendor, between the little sparkling stars of infant souls and the effulgent orb of the Queen of Heaven, is gained by each one who endures and conquers. "*To him that overcometh, I will give him the* *hidden manna, and I will give him a white stone, and on the white stone a new name written, which no one knoweth but he who receiveth. He who shall overcome and keep my works unto the end, I will give him power over the nations ; and I will give him the morning star. He who shall overcome shall be clothed with white robes, and I will not blot out his name from the book of life, and I will own his name before my Father, and before his angels. Him that shall overcome, I will make a pillar in the temple of my God, and he shall not go out any more ; and I will write on him the name of my God, and the name of the city of my God, the new Jerusalem, which cometh down out of heaven from my God, and my new name. To him who shall overcome, I will give to sit down with me in my throne, as I also overcame, and sat down with my Father in his throne."**

Without excluding the minor and ac-

---

*Apoc. ii. 17, 26, 28 ; iii. 5, 12, 21.

cidental glories represented by these sublime metaphors, the chief and supreme good which is set forth by them, in a hidden manner, is the vision of God. The increase of glory is an increase of this vision, a closer and more elevated union with God, a greater capacity of loving him and being loved by him, a nearer approach to the union which subsists between the Son and the Father. This is the divine life which is begun on earth in purified souls. Whoever will be faithful to God, therefore, in the obscure night of this life, during which He cannot be seen, must rise above everything, and put aside everything which is not the immediate union of the soul with God himself, in pure, disinterested love. This can only be exercised by that kind of prayer which is fitted to bring the soul into interior, recollected, and truly spiritual contemplation of that which is revealed of God by faith. Suitable spiritual books are also necessary, as guides and companions to this prayer. In this treatise I have aimed to give inexperienced persons an introduction to books of this kind, and to prepare them to make use of them with docility, discretion, and profit. I have already recommended those which are the best and most suitable; and among these, I recommend, in conclusion, as a practical guide to those who are resolved to walk in the way I have pointed out, the *Sancta Sophia* of F. Baker. The directions there given for the practice of various kinds of mental prayer are those which are the most suitable, and fully sufficient for that class of persons for whom I have written this little book. The *Parable of the Pilgrim* contains, in brief, the whole doctrine I have endeavored to set forth, and a summary of the whole Christian life of those who seek to take the most direct road to heaven. The rest of the book gives plain and wise directions and instructions in regard to every matter of practical importance. In fact, were it not for our instability of mind, our capriciousness of taste, and the need we have of a variety and change of spiritual food, whoever would study this book carefully, and endeavor to put its instructions assiduously into practice, would need no other book during his whole life. I have borrowed a little light from this holy Benedictine, from the great glory of Carmel, St. John of the Cross, and from other holy men who were enlightened of God, in order to cast a ray upon the path of those who have been walking in darkness. This ray of light, if they follow it, will direct them where to find the Teacher and Comforter who is present within their own souls, and who is to be sought by silence, by solitude, by recollection, and by the interior life. If you find him, O soul! beloved in God, who have sought consolation in this little book, you will have small need of any human counsel for the future; and if not, you will find small benefit or comfort from any human source whatever. I commend you to God, and I leave you with God. May he give you peace, and a quiet night. Noctem quietam et finem perfectum, concedat nobis Dominus omnipotens. Amen.*

* May the Almighty Lord grant us a quiet night and a perfect end. Amen.—*Office of Compline.*

JOHN ROSS & CO., PRINTERS, 27 ROSE STREET, NEW YORK.

THE

CATHOLIC PUBLICATION SOCIETY'S

BOOKS.

Abridgment of the Christian Doctrine. By the Right
Rev. Bishop Hay. 32mo, cloth, ... $0 25

An Amicable Discussion on the Church of England,
and on the Reformation in General. Dedicated to the
Clergy of every Protestant Communion, and reduced into
the form of letters by the Right Rev. J. F. M. Trevern,
D.D., Bishop of Strasbourg. Translated by the Rev. Wm.
Richmond. 1 vol. 12mo, 580 pp., ... $2 00

An Illustrated History of Ireland, from the Earliest
Period to the Present Time ; with several first-class full-page
Engravings of Historical Scenes, designed by Henry Doyle,
and engraved by George Hanlon and George Pearson ; together with upwards of 100 woodcuts, by eminent artists,
illustrating Antiquities, Scenery, and Sites of Remarkable
Events ; and three large maps, one of Ireland and the others
of Family Homes, Statistics, etc. 1 vol. 8vo, nearly 700 pp.
New and enlarged edition. Extra cloth, $5 00 ; half calf, $7 00

Anima Divota ; or, Devout Soul. Translated from the
Italian of Very Rev. J. B. Pagani, Provincial of the Order
of Charity in England. 24mo, cloth, ... $0 60

Anne Severin. By the Author of "A Sister's Story." 1 vol.
12mo, cloth, $1 50 ; cloth, gilt, ... $2 00

Apologia pro Vita Sua : Being a Reply to a Pamphlet en
titled "What, then, does Dr. Newman Mean?" By John
Henry Newman, D.D. New edition. 1 vol. 12mo, $2 00

A Sister's Story. By Mrs. Augustus Craven. Translated
from the French by Emily Bowles. 1 vol. crown 8vo, pp.
558. Cloth, extra, $2 50 ; vellum cloth, gilt, . $3 00

Aspirations of Nature. By Rev. I. T. Hecker. 4th edi
tion, revised cloth, extra, ... $1 50

Beauties of Sir Thomas More. A Selection from his Works, as well in prose as in verse. A sequel to " Life and Times of More." By W. J. Walter. 18mo, cloth, . $1 25

Bona Mors. A Pious Association of the Devout Servants of our Lord Jesus Christ dying on the Cross in order to obtain a Good Death. 24mo, cloth, ... $0 25

Catechism of Council of Trent. 8vo, . . . $2 00

Catholic Christian Instructed. By the Right Rev. Dr. Challoner. 24mo, flexible cloth, $0 25; extra cloth, $0 40

The Same. 12mo, large type, flexible cloth, $0 50; extra cloth, ... $0 75

Catholic Manual; containing a Selection of Prayers and Devotional Exercises. 18mo, embossed, $1 00; roan, 2 plates, $1 50; roan, gilt edge, 4 plates, $1 75; turkey morocco, super extra, 8 plates, ... $3 00

Christian's Guide to Heaven. 32mo, cloth, $0 50; roan, 4 engravings, $0 60; roan, gilt edge, 4 engravings, $1 00; turkey, super extra, 6 engravings, . . . $2 50

Christine and Other Poems. By George H. Miles. Illustrated, ... $2 00

Compendious Abstract of the History of the Church of Christ. By Rev. Wm. Gahan. 12mo, . . . $1 00

Confidence in the Mercy of God. By the Right Rev. Joseph Languet. 18mo, cloth, ... $0 50

Cradle Lands: Egypt, Palestine, etc. By Lady Herbert. 1 vol. 12mo, vellum cloth, $2 00; cloth, gilt, $2 50; half calf, $4 00; full calf, red edges, ... $6 00

Daily Companion; containing a Selection of Prayers and Devotional Exercises for the Use of Children. Embellished with 36 very neat illustrative engravings. 32mo, cloth, $0 25; roan, ... $0 60

Defence of Catholic Principles. By the Rev. D. A. Gallitzin. 4th edition, 18mo, cloth, ... $0 60

Devout Communicant. By the Rev. P. Baker. New edition, 24mo, cloth, $0 60; roan, $1 25; roan, gilt edges, $1 75; turkey morocco, super extra, ... $3 00

Douay Bible. 12mo, suitable for Missionaries. Embellished, ... $1 50

Douay Testament. A beautiful pocket edition. 32mo, cloth, $0 45; roan, embossed, $0 60; roan, embossed, gilt edges, $1 00; tuck, gilt edges, $1 25; fine edition, roan, $1 00; fine edition, roan, gilt edge, $1 50; fine edition, turkey morocco, super extra $2 25

Douay Testament. 12mo large type, embellished, . $0 75

Epistle of Jesus Christ to the Faithful Soul, . $1 00

Eugenie de Guerin, Journal of, ... $2 00

Eugenie de Guerin, Letters of, ... $2 00

Exposition of the Doctrine of the Catholic Church in Matters of Controversy. By the Right Rev. J. B. Bossuet. A new edition, with copious notes, by Rev. J. Fletcher, D.D. 18mo, $0 60 ; another edition, without notes, 32mo, cloth, ... $0 25

Father Rowland. A North American Tale. 18mo, cloth, $0 60

Following of Christ. In four books. By Thomas à Kempis with Reflections at the conclusion of each Chapter. 18mo, cloth, $0 50 ; roan, plates, $1 50 ; roan, gilt edge, plates, $1 75 ; turkey morocco, super extra, ... $3 00

The Same. Pocket edition, without the Reflections, 32mo, cloth, $0 25 ; roan, $0 60 ; roan, gilt edge, $1 00 ; turkey morocco, super extra, ... $2 50

Garden of the Soul ; or, A Manual of Spiritual Exercises and Instructions for Christians, who, living in the world, aspire to devotion. By Right Rev. Dr. Challoner. 24mo, arabesque, $0 50 ; roan, 2 plates, $0 75 ; roan, gilt edges, 4 plates, $1 00 ; turkey, super extra, 8 plates, . . $3 50

Genevieve : A Tale of Antiquity, showing the Wonderful Ways of Providence in the Protection of Innocence. From the German of Schmid. 18mo, cloth, . . . $0 60

Glimpses of Pleasant Homes. By the Author of "The Life of Mother McCauley." Illustrated with four full-page illustrations. 1 vol. 12mo, cloth, extra, $1 50 ; cloth, gilt, $2 00

Gropings after Truth : A Life-Journey from New England Congregationalism to the One Catholic Apostolic Church. By Joshua Huntington. 1 vol. vellum cloth, . . $0 75

Grounds of the Catholic Doctrine, contained in the Profession of Faith. Published by Pope Pius IV. 32mo, cloth, $0 20

Historical Catechism. By M. l'Abbé Fleury. Parts I. and II., revised by Right Rev. Bishop Cheverus. 18mo, paper cover, $0 12 ; complete, in four parts, 18mo, . $0 60

History of England, for the Use of Schools, to the end of the Reign of George IV. By W. F. Mylius. 12mo, $1 00

History of the Church from its Establishment to the Reformation. By Rev. C. C. Pise. 5 vols. 8vo, $7 50 ; another edition, 5 vols. 12mo, cloth, ... $5 00

History of the Old and New Testaments. By J. Reeve. 8vo, half-bound, roan, ... $1 00

Hornihold. The Commandments and Sacraments Explained in Fifty-two Discourses. By the Right Rev. Dr. Hornihold, author of " Real Principles of Catholics." 12mo, cloth, $2 00

Home of the Lost Child. 18mo, cloth, . . . $0 60

Homilies on the Book of Tobias ; or, A Familiar Explanation of the Practical Duties of Domestic Life. By Rev. T. Martyn. 12mo, cloth, ... $0 75

Hours of the Passion ; or, Pathetic Reflections on the Suf ˞ ings and Death of our Blessed Redeemer. By St. Ligu ʌ. New edition, translated by Right Rev. W. Walsh, Late Bishop of Halifax. 18mo, cloth, ... $0 60

Imitation of the Blessed Virgin. In four books. 18mo, cloth, ... $0 60

Impressions of Spain. By Lady Herbert. 1 vol. 12mo. 15 illustrations. Cloth, extra, $2 00 ; cloth, gilt, $2 50 ; half morocco, or calf, $4 00 ; full calf, ... $6 00

In Heaven we know Our Own, ... $0 60

Interior Christian. In eight books, with a supplement ; extracted from the writings of M. Bernier de Louvigny. 18mo, cloth, ... $0 60

Introduction to a Devout Life. From the French of St. Francis of Sales. 18mo, cloth, ... $0 75

Irish Odes and Other Poems. By Aubrey de Vere. 1 vol. 12mo, toned paper, $2 00 ; cloth, gilt, . . $2 50

Key of Paradise, opening the Gate to Eternal Salvation. 18mo, arabesque, $1 00 ; roan, 2 plates, $1 50 ; roan, gilt edge, 4 plates, $1 75 ; turkey morocco, super extra, 8 plates, ... $3 50

Lenten Monitor ; or, Moral Reflections and Devout Aspirations on the Gospel. By Rev. P. Baker, O. S. F. 24mo, cloth, New edition, ... $0 60

Letters to a Prebendary. Being an Answer to "Reflections on Popery," by Rev. J. Sturgis, LL.D. By Right Rev. J. Milner, D.D. 24mo, cloth, ... $0 60

Letters to a Protestant Friend on the Holy Scriptures. By Rev. D. A. Gallitzin. 18mo, cloth, . . . $0 60

Life and Times of Sir Thomas More, Illustrated from his Own Writings. By W. J. Walter. With a portrait and autograph of More. 18mo, cloth, ... $1 25

Life of St. Catharine of Sienna, ... $1 75

Life of St. Vincent de Paul. 32mo, cloth, . . $0 45

Little Treatise on the Little Virtues. Written originally in Italian, by Father Roberti, of the Society of Jesus. To which are added, "A Letter on Fervor," by Father Vallois, S J., and "Maxims," from an unpublished manuscript of Father Segneri, S. J. ; also, "Devotions to the Sacred Heart of Jesus." 32mo, cloth, ... $0 45

Lives of the Fathers of the Desert, and of many Holy Men and Women who Dwelt in Solitude. Translated from the French. Embellished with 18 engravings. 18mo, cloth, $0 60

Louisa ; or, The Virtuous Villager. A Catholic Tale. New edition. 18mo, cloth, ... $0 60

Love of our Lord Jesus Christ reduced to Practice. By St. Alphonsus Liguori. Translated by the Right Rev. W.

Walsh, late Bishop of Halifax. New edition, 8mo, cloth, ... $0 60

Way Carols, and Hymns and Poems. By Aubrey de Vere. Blue and gold, ... $1 25

Memorial of a Christian Life. By Rev. Lewis de Granada. Revised edition. 18mo, cloth, ... $0 75

Memorials of those who Suffered for the Catholic Faith in Ireland during the Sixteenth, Seventeenth, and Eighteenth Centuries. Collected and edited by Myles O'Reilly, B.A., LL.D. 1 vol. crown 8vo, vellum cloth, $2 50 ; cloth, gilt, $3 00 ; half calf, ... $4 50

Month of Mary, containing a Series of Meditations, etc., in honor of the B. V. M. Arranged for each day of the month. 32mo, cloth, ... $0 40

Nellie Netterville ; or, One of the Transplanted. A Tale of the Times of Cromwell in Ireland. 1 vol. 12mo, cloth, extra, $1 50 ; cloth, gilt, ... $2 00

Net for the Fishers of Men, ... $0 06

Nouet. Meditations on the Life and Passion of our Lord Jesus Christ for every Day in the Year. By Rev. J. Nouet, S. J. To which are added, "Meditations on the Sacred Heart of Jesus Christ," being those taken from a Nouvena in preparation for the Feast of the same. By Father C. Borgo, S. J. 1 vol. 12mo, 880 pp., ... $2 50

Office of the Holy Week, according to the Roman Missal and Breviary, in Latin and English. 18mo, cloth, $0 75 ; roan, 1 plate, $1 50 ; roan, gilt edge, 2 plates, $2 00 ; turkey morocco, super extra, 4 plates, ... $3 50

O'Kane. Notes on the Rubrics of the Roman Ritual. 1 vol. 12mo, ... $4 00

Oratory of the Faithful Soul ; or, Devotions to the Most Holy Sacrament and to our Blessed Lady. Translated from the works of Ven. Abbot Blosius. By Robert Aston Coffin. 18mo, cloth, ... $0 50

Packets of Scripture Illustrations. Containing 50 engravings of subjects from the Old and New Testaments, after original designs by Elster. Loose packages of 50, $0 75

Path to Paradise. A Selection of Prayers and Devotions for Catholics. 48mo, cloth, $0 20 ; roan, $0 40 ; roan, gilt edge, $0 60 ; turkey morocco, sup. extra, 4 engravings, $1 50

Pious Guide to Prayer and Devotion. Containing various Practices of Piety, calculated to Answer the Demands of the Devout Members of the Catholic Church. 18mo, arabesque, $1 00 ; roan, 2 plates, $1 50 ; roan, gilt edge, 4 plates, $1 75 ; turkey morocco, super extra, 8 plates, $3 50 ; various styles in velvet and turkey morocco, with clasps and ornaments, from $4 50 to $10 00. A new and beautiful edition, containing the same as the above large edition

24mo, arabesque, $3 60; roan, 2 plates, $. 00; roan, gilt
edge, 4 plates, $1 50; turkey morocco, super extra, 8
plates, ... $3 00

Poor Man's Catechism; or, The Christian Doctrine Explained, with Short Admonitions. By John Mannock, O.S.B.
24mo, cloth, ... $3 50

Poor Man's Manual of Devotion; or, Devout Christian's
Daily Companion. To which is added, "Daily Devotion;
or, Profitable Manner of Hearing Mass." 24mo, arabesque,
$0 50; roan, $0 80; roan, gilt edge, $1 50; turkey, super
extra, ... $2 50

Poor Man's Controversy. By J. Mannock, Author of
" Poor Man's Catechism." 18mo, cloth, . . . $0 50

Practical Discourses on the Perfections and Works of God,
and the Divinity and Works of Jesus Christ. By the Rev.
J. Reeve. 8vo, cloth, ... $2 00

Problems of the Age, with Studies in St. Augustine on
Kindred Topics. By Rev. Augustine F. Hewit. 1 vol.
12mo, cloth, extra, ... $2 00

Questions of the Soul. By Rev. I. T. Hecker. New edition, $1 50; cloth, gilt, ... $2 00

Reason and Revelation. Lectures delivered in St. Ann's
Church, New York, during Advent, 1867. By Rev. T. S.
Preston. 1 vol. 12mo, ... $1 50

Sacred Heart of Jesus and the Sacred Heart of Mary.
Translated from the Italian of Father Lanzi, Author of
" History of Painting," etc., with an introduction by Rev.
C. B. Mechan. 24mo, cloth, ... $0 60

St. Columba, Apostle of Caledonia. By the Count de
Montalembert. 1 vol. 12mo. Toned paper, $1 25; cloth,
gilt, ... $1 75

*Sermons of the Paulist Fathers for the Years 1865
and 1866,* $1 50

Sermons of the Paulist Fathers for the Year 1864.
New edition, ... $1 50

Short Treatise on Prayer, adapted to all Classes of Christians. By St. Alphonsus Liguori. New edition, 24mo,
cloth, ... $0 40

Spirit of St. Alphonsus de Liguori. A Selection from
his shorter Spiritual Treatises. Translated by the Rev. J.
Jones. 24mo, cloth, ... $0 60

Spiritual Combat. To which is added, "The Peace of the
Soul and the Happiness of the Heart which Dies to Itself in
Order to Live to God." 32mo, ... $0 40

Spiritual Consoler; or, Instructions to Enlighten Pious Souls
in their Doubts, etc. By Father Quadrupani. 18mo, $0 50

Spiritual Director of Devout and Religious Souls. **By** St. Francis de Sales, ... $0 50

Stories on the Seven Virtues. By Agnes M. Stewart, Authoress of "Festival of the Rosary." 18mo, cloth, . $0 60

Symbolism; or, Exposition of the Doctrinal Differences between Catholics and Protestants, as evidenced by their Symbolical Writings. By John A. Moehler, D.D. Translated from the German, with a Memoir of the Author, preceded by an Historical Sketch of the State of Protestantism and Catholicism in Germany for the last Hundred Years, by J. B. Robertson, Esq., ... $4 00

Tales from the Diary of a Sister of Mercy. By C. M. Brame. 1 vol. 12mo, cloth, extra, $1 50; cloth, gilt, $2 00

The Clergy and the Pulpit, in their Relations to the People. By M. l'Abbe Isidore Mullois, Chaplain to Napoleon III. 1 vol. 12mo, extra cloth, ... $1 50

The Comedy of Convocation in the English Church. In Two Scenes. Edited by Archdeacon Chasuble, D.D., and dedicated to the Pan-Anglican Synod. 8vo pamphlet. Paper, $0 75; bound in cloth, ... $1 00

The Holy Communion: Its Philosophy, Theology, and Practice. By John Bernard Dalgairns, Priest of the Oratory of Saint Philip Neri. 1 vol. 12mo, . . . $2 00

The Illustrated Catholic Sunday-School Library. 1st Series. 12 vols. handsomely bound, and put up in a box. Cloth, extra, $6 00; cloth, gilt, ... $7 50

The Illustrated Catholic Sunday-School Library. 2d Series. 12 vols. handsomely bound in cloth, put up in a box. Cloth, extra, $6 00; cloth, gilt, ... $7 50

The Illustrated Catholic Sunday-School Library. 3d Series. 12 vols. in box. Cloth, extra, $6 00; gilt, . $7 50

The Inner Life of the Very Rev. Pere Lacordaire, of the Order of Preachers. Translated from the French of the Rev. Pere Chocarne, O. P. By a Father of the same Order; with Preface by Father Aylward, Prior Provincial of England. 1 vol. 12mo, toned paper, ... $3 00

The Life and Sermons of the Rev. Francis A. Baker, Priest of the Congregation of St. Paul. Edited by Rev. A. F. Hewit. 1 vol. crown 8vo, pp. 504. $2 50; half calf, $4 00

The Life of Father Ravignan, S. J. By Father Ponlevoy, S. J. 1 vol. crown 8vo, toned paper, . . $4 00

The People's Pictorial Lives of the Saints, Scriptural and Historical. Abridged, for the most part, from those of the late Rev. Alban Butler. These are got up expressly for Sunday-school presents. In packets of 12 each. One packet now ready, containing the lives of twelve different saints. Per packet, ... $0 25

The See of St. Peter. The Rock of the Church, the Source of Jurisdiction, and Centre of Unity. By Thomas William Allies, M.A. 1 vol. 16mo, ... $0 75

The Two Schools. A Moral Tale. By Mrs. Hughs. 12mo, cloth, ... $1 00

The Works of the Most Rev. John Hughes, D.D., First Archbishop of New York, containing Biography, Sermons, Letters, Lectures, Speeches, etc. Carefully compiled from the best sources, and edited by Lawrence Kehoe. This important work makes 2 large vols. of nearly 1,500 pp. 8vo. Cloth, $6 00 ; half calf, extra, ... $12 00

Think Well On't ; or, The Great Truths of the Christian Religion for Every Day in the Month. By Right Rev. R. Challoner. 32mo, cloth, ... $0 25

Three Phases of Christian Love : The Mother, the Maiden, and the Religious. By Lady Herbert. 1 vol. 12mo, vellum cloth, $1 50 ; gilt, ... $2 00

Triumph of Religion ; or, A Choice Selection of Edifying Narratives. 18mo, cloth, ... $0 60

True Piety ; or, The Day Well Spent. A Manual of Fervent Prayers, Pious Reflections, and Solid Instructions for the Members of the Catholic Church. 18mo, arabesque, $1 00 ; roan, 2 plates, $1 50 ; roan, gilt edge, 4 plates, $1 75 ; turkey morocco, super extra, 8 plates, . . . $3 50

Visits to the Blessed Sacrament and to the Blessed Virgin for Every Day in the Month. By St. Alphonsus Liguori. 24mo, cloth. New edition, . . . $0 60

Way of Salvation. Meditations for Every Day in the Year. By St. Alphonsus Liguori. 24mo, cloth, . . . $0 75

Why Men do not Believe; or, The Principal Causes of Infidelity. Translated from the French of Mgr. Laforet. Cloth, ... $1 00

Any Book on this List sent by mail, post-paid on receipt of the advertised price.

The Catholic Publication Society,

LAWRENCE KEHOE, General Agent,

No. 9 WARREN STREET. NEW YORK.